Esther Suhha Lee
780·695·6814

SHEPHERDING
A CHILD'S
HEART

Esther Sukha free
780. 695. 6814

SHEPHERDING
A CHILD'S
HEART

Revised and Updated

Second Edition

TEDD TRIPP

Shepherd Press
Wapwallopen, PA

Shepherding A Child's Heart

©1995 by Tedd Tripp

ISBN 0-9663786-0-1 (previously ISBN 1-879737-19-1)

Second Edition 2005

Unless otherwise noted, Scripture quotations are from the *New International Version* (NIV), ©1994 International Bible Society. Italic text indicates emphasis added.

Design and composition by Lakeside Design Plus
Cover design by Tobias Outerwear for Books

Manufactured in the United States of America

To Margy:
Whose help and support
enabled me both to learn
and to write what is found herein.

CONTENTS

PREFACE TO THE SECOND EDITION

*I*N THE TEN YEARS since *Shepherding a Child's Heart* was published I have taught the material in this book hundreds of times. I have conversed with scores of young people who are in the throes of childrearing. These opportunities have left me more and more convinced of some biblical underpinnings that are essential for making sense of the childrearing task.

God is concerned with the heart—the well-spring of life (Proverbs 4:23). Parents tend to focus on the externals of behavior rather than the internal overflow of the heart. We tend to worry more about the "what" of behavior than the "why". Accordingly, most of us spend an enormous amount of energy in controlling and constraining behavior. To the degree and extent to which our focus is on behavior, we miss the heart.

When we miss the heart, we miss the subtle idols of the heart. Romans 1 makes it clear that all human beings are worshipers; either we worship and serve God, or we make an exchange and worship and serve substitutes for God—created things rather than the Creator (Romans 1:18-25). When parenting short-circuits to behavior we miss the opportunity to help our kids understand that straying behavior displays a straying heart. Our kids are always serving something, either God or a substitute for God—an idol of the heart.

When we miss the heart, we miss the gospel. If the goal of parenting is no more profound than securing appropriate behavior, we will never help our children understand the internal things, the heart issues, that push and pull behavior. Those internal issues: self-love, rebellion, anger, bitterness, envy, and pride of the heart show our children how profoundly they need grace. If the problem with children is deeper than inappropriate behavior, if the problem is the overflow of the heart, then the need for grace is established. Jesus came to earth, lived a perfect life and died as an infinite sacrifice so that children (and their parents) can be forgiven, transformed, liberated and empowered to love God and love others.

When we miss the heart, we miss the glory of God. The need of children (or adults) who have fallen into various forms of personal idolatry is not only to tear down the high places of the alien gods, but to enthrone God. Children are spring-loaded for worship. One of the most important callings God has given parents is to display the greatness, goodness, and glory of the God for whom they are made. Parents have the opportunity, through word and deed, to show children the one true object of worship—the God of the Bible. We know that the greatest delights our children can ever experience are found in delighting in the God who has made them for his glory.

Many times when I have taught the things found in this book people have come to me and said, "These truths you are teaching are not just about our children; they are about me." We need to incarnate these truths for our children.

So, welcome to the second edition of *Shepherding a Child's Heart*. What you find here may be a paradigm shift for you, but it will bear good fruit in your life and in the lives of your children.

My prayer for you is expressed by King David in Psalm 78, that not only would you teach and model these truths for your children, but that even generations yet unborn would arise and teach them to their children, so they might put their hope in God.

Tedd Tripp
July, 2005

PREFACE TO THE FIRST EDITION

I HAVE BEEN MOTIVATED to write on this subject because I believe that our culture, and therefore the church, is in great need of a biblical focus on the task of parenting.

I have sought to apply the principles which I have seen bear good fruit in my life and in the counseling and pastoral ministry God has given me.

Thanks are in order. My family has been of great support throughout this arduous writing process. It is no easy task for a preacher to become a writer. My dear wife Margy has read this book more times than either of us care to remember. If you think it is too long, you should thank her for chopping words as she did her "Strunk and White" simplification several times. My now-adult children, Tedd, Heather and Aaron, have been willing to be named and analyzed as illustrations. Tedd's wife, Heather, has been a willing and valuable help in the final steps before publication. Their vitality and ardent love for God has encouraged me many times when I would have given up in this task.

The people of Grace Fellowship Church, whom I have loved and learned from for 21 years, have had great influence on my walk with God as well as on the content of this book. They have helped me refine the things taught here through countless times of teaching. My fellow elders and the deacons who serve us faithfully have encouraged me to "get away" to work on this on many occasions when I would have let the project die.

There have been many faithful readers: Daniel Boehret, Gene Cannon, Marcia Ciszek, Jon and Jose Hueni, Kelly Knowlden, Jean Neel, Ted Vinatieri, and Jay and Ruth Younts. The cogent comments and observations of these people have clarified and focused the content.

A special thanks to David Powlison and Jay E. Adams of the Christian Counseling and Educational Foundation. David's teaching is a model of true spirituality I have sought to emulate and apply to the task of childrearing. Jay Adams has sharpened me "like iron sharpens iron." I am in his debt.

May God bless these things to raising up a holy seed for his church.

Tedd Tripp
July 1995

FOREWORD

THIS IS A MASTERFUL BOOK. Tedd Tripp knows what he is talking about and he knows whom he is talking to. He knows children, he knows parents . . . and he knows the ways of God.

Most books on parenting give you advice either on how to shape and constrain your children's behavior or on how to make them feel good about themselves. Either control or self-actualization is deemed the goal of parenting. The former makes parental wishes supreme; the latter makes childish wishes supreme.

Shepherding a Child's Heart contains something very different. The book teaches you what your goals as a parent ought to be, and how to pursue those ends practically. It teaches you how to engage children about what really matters, how to address your child's heart by your words and actions. It teaches you how communication and discipline work together when parents love wisely. It teaches you how your objectives shift as infants grow into children and as children grow into teenagers. *Shepherding a Child's Heart* will humble you. It will inspire you to become a different kind of parent. It will teach you how by precept and example.

Most books on parenting actually don't understand what children—or parents—are really like. Their advice builds on a foundation untrue to Scripture, untrue to human reality. Their bits of good advice mingle with bits of bad advice because the overarching vision is faulty; their bits of good advice totter or misfire because the balancing elements of wise parenting are neglected. Tedd Tripp's book on parenting is different. The cornerstone is accurately aligned. *Shepherding a Child's Heart* understands you and your children truly, so it leads in straight and wise paths. Tripp gives you a vision and he makes it practical. You can't ask for more.

Tedd Tripp is a seasoned parent, pastor, counselor, and school principal. But more than that, he is a man who has listened well to God and has wrestled out what it means to raise children. Listen well to him, and wrestle out what it means to shepherd your child's heart.

David Powlison
Christian Counseling and
Educational Foundation
Laverock, PA

INTRODUCTION

JENNIFER WAS FAILING to do her homework. Her teacher called Jennifer's folks to solicit help. But her parents could not help. Twelve-year-old Jennifer would not obey them. Jennifer was not under their authority. They had hoped that school would provide the direction and motivation they had not been able to provide for their daughter.

This story is not unusual. By age ten to twelve, scores of children have already left home. I am not referring to the tragic "Times Square kids" in New York City or your community. I refer to numbers of children who, by age ten to twelve, have effectively left Mom or Dad as an authority or reference point for their lives.

Our culture has lost its way with respect to parenting. We are a rudderless ship without a compass. We lack both a sense of direction and the capacity to direct ourselves.

How has this happened? Several problems have converged at this intersection in our time and culture.

Many people have children, but do not want to be parents. Our culture has convinced them that they need to quench their personal thirst for fulfillment. In a self-absorbed culture, children are a clear liability.

Thus, parents spend minimal time with their children. The notion of quality time is more attractive than the old idea of quantity time.

Today's parents are part of the generation that threw off authority. The racial and antiwar protests of the 1960s powerfully shaped their ideas. The protest movement took on the establishment. It changed the way we think about authority and the rights of the individual.

As a result, it is no longer culturally acceptable for Dad to be the "boss" at home. Mom doesn't obediently do what Dad says, or at least pretend she does. Dad, for his part, no longer lives in fear of the boss or of being fired through caprice. Yesterday's bosses used authority to accomplish their goals. Today's bosses use bonuses and incentives.

What is my point? Simply this: Children raised in this climate no longer sit in neat rows in school. They no longer ask permission to speak. They no longer fear the consequences of talking back to their parents. They do not accept a submissive role in life.

How does this bear on parenting? The old ways of parenting no longer work. Old authoritarian ways are ineffective, but we do not know any new ways to do the job.

The church borrowed the old "you listen to me, kid, or I'll cuff you" method of raising children. It seemed to work. Children seemed to obey. They were externally submissive. This method fails us now because our culture no longer responds to authority as it did a generation ago. We lament the passing of this way of rearing children because we miss its simplicity. I fear, however, we have overlooked its unbiblical methods and goals.

Today's parents are frustrated and confused. Children don't act like they should and parents don't understand why. Many have concluded the job is impossible. Some simply turn away in frustration. Others keep trying to make the old 1950s John Wayne approach work. Meanwhile, a generation of children is being wasted.

Our evangelical culture is nearly as lost as the society at large. We are losing our children. Parents of little children live in mortal fear of adolescence. Parents of teens continually remind them that their day is coming. When I had three teenage children, people would console me. The expectation is that the problems grow with the children.

This book, however, asserts hope for the situation. You can raise children in godly ways at the beginning of the 21st century. You need not—indeed, you dare not—cave in, concluding that the task is impossible. Experience may tell you failure is inevitable, but experience is an unsafe guide.

The only safe guide is the Bible. It is the revelation of a God who has infinite knowledge and can therefore give you absolute truth. God has given you a revelation that is robust and complete. It presents an accurate and comprehensive picture of children, parents, family life, values, training, nurture, and discipline—all you need to be equipped for the task of parenting.

God's ways have not proved inadequate; they are simply untried. The church mirrors the problems of the culture because we weren't doing biblical parenting a generation ago. We were just doing what worked. Unfortunately, we are still trying to do it, even though, because of changes in our culture, it no longer works.

Let me overview a biblical vision for the parenting task. The parenting task is multifaceted. It involves being a kind authority, shepherding your children to understand themselves in God's world, and keeping the gospel in clear view so your children can internalize the good news and someday live in mutuality with you as people under God.

Authority

God calls his creatures to live under authority. He is our authority and has vested authority in people within the institutions he has established (home, church, state, and business). You must not be embarrassed to be authorities for your children.

You exercise authority as God's agent. You may not direct your children for your own agenda or convenience. You must direct your children on God's behalf for their good.

Our culture tends toward the extreme poles on a continuum. In the area of authority, we tend either toward a crass kind of John Wayne authoritarianism or toward being a wimp. God calls you by his Word and his example to be authorities who are truly kind. God calls you to exercise authority, not in making your children do what you want, but in being true servants—authorities who lay down your lives. The purpose for your authority in the lives of your children is not to hold them under your power, but to empower them to be self-controlled people living freely under the authority of God.

Jesus is an example of this. The One who commands you, the One who possesses all authority, came as a servant. He is a ruler who serves; he is also a servant who rules. He exercises sovereign authority that is kind—authority exercised on behalf of his subjects. In John 13, Jesus, who knew that the Father had put all things under his authority, put on a towel and washed the disciples' feet. As his people submit to his authority, they are empowered to live freely in the freedom of the gospel.

As a parent, you must exercise authority. You must require obedience of your children because they are called by God to obey and honor you. You must exercise authority, not as a cruel taskmaster, but as one who truly loves them.

Parents who are "benevolent despots" do not usually find their children racing to leave home. Children rarely run from a home where their needs are met. Who would want to walk out on a relationship in which he feels loved and respected? What child would run from someone who understands him, understands God and his ways, understands the world and how it works, and is committed to helping him be successful?

My observation after thirty-five years of school administration, parenting, pastoral work, and counseling is that children generally do not resist authority that is truly kind and selfless.

Shepherding

If authority best describes the parent's relationship to the child, the best description of the activity of the parent to the child is shepherding. The parent is the child's guide. This shepherding process helps a child to understand himself and the world in which he lives. The parent shepherds a child to assess himself and his responses. He shepherds the child to understand not just the "what" of the child's actions, but also the "why." As the shepherd, you want to help your child understand himself as a creature made by and for God. You cannot show him these things merely by instruction; you must lead him on a path of discovery. You must shepherd his thoughts, helping him to learn discernment and wisdom.

This shepherding process is a richer interaction than telling your child what to do and think. It involves investing your life in your child in open and honest communication that unfolds the meaning and purpose of life. It is not simply direction, but direction in which there is self-disclosure and sharing. Values and spiritual vitality are not simply taught, but caught.

Proverbs 13:20 says, "He who walks with the wise becomes wise." As a wise parent your objective is not simply to discuss, but to demonstrate the freshness and vitality of life lived in integrity toward God and your family. Parenting is shepherding the hearts of your children in the ways of God's wisdom.

The Centrality of the Gospel

People frequently ask if I expected my children to become believers. I usually reply that the gospel is powerful and attractive. It uniquely meets the needs of fallen humanity. Therefore, I expected that God's Word would be the power of God to salvation for my children. But that expectation was based on the power of the gospel and its suitability to human need, not on a correct formula for producing children who believe.

The central focus of parenting is the gospel. You need to direct not simply the behavior of your children, but the attitudes of their hearts. You need to show them not just the "what" of their sin and failure, but the "why." Your children desperately need to understand not only the external "what" they did wrong, but also the internal "why" they did it. You must help them see that God works from the inside out. Therefore, your parenting goal cannot simply be well behaved children. Your children must also understand why they sin and how to recognize internal change.

Keeping the gospel in focus, you see, is more than helping our children know forgiveness of sin through repentance and faith in Jesus Christ. In the gospel there is the promise of internal transformation and empowerment. Ezekiel 36 expresses well the fullness of the gospel, *(verse 25) I will sprinkle clean water on you, and you will be clean; I will cleanse you from all your impurities and from all your idols.* The grace of forgiveness is found in the gospel. *(26) I will give you a new heart and put a new spirit in you; I will remove from you your heart of stone and give you a heart of flesh.* The grace of internal change is found in the gospel. *(27) And I will put my Spirit in you and move you to follow my decrees and be careful to keep my laws.* The grace of empowerment to live is found in the gospel. The gospel enables you and your children to face the worst in yourselves—your sin, your badness, and your weakness—and still find hope, because grace is powerful.

Parents sometimes give children a keepable standard. Parents think that if their children aren't Christians, they can't obey God from the heart anyway. For example, the Bible says to do good to those who mistreat you. But when children are bullied in the schoolyard, parents tell them to ignore the bully. Or worse, parents tell them to hit others when they are hit first.

This non-biblical counsel drives children away from the cross. It doesn't take grace from God to ignore the oppressor. It doesn't take supernatural grace to stand up for your rights. To do good to oppressors, however, to pray for those who mistreat you, to entrust yourself to the just Judge, requires a child to come face-to-face with the poverty of his own spirit and his need of the transforming power of the gospel.

The law of God is not easy for natural man. Its standard is high and cannot be achieved apart from God's supernatural grace. God's law teaches us our need of grace. When you fail to hold out God's standard, you rob your children of the mercy of the gospel.

Internalization of the Gospel

Ultimately, your children must internalize the message of the gospel. Each child in a Christian home will at some point examine the claims of the gospel and determine whether he will embrace its truth. Picture the process this way: The child holds the claims of the gospel at arm's length, turning it in his hand and determining either to embrace it or to cast it away.

The parent has a marvelous opportunity to help his young adult child pursue with honesty all his questions of faith. The Word of God is robust; Christian faith can withstand close, honest scrutiny. Everyone does not have the obligation to ask every question, but everyone has the obligation to ask every question that he has.

Mutuality as People under God

I recently had a conversation with my son. He was talking to me about the things God was teaching him. He shared new insights into himself and what it means to know God in more than theoretical ways.

As we talked together it seemed that I was talking not just with my son, but with another man. I wasn't instructing him. We were sharing the goodness of knowing God. I felt a wonderful sense of mutuality with this man (who was once a boy whom I instructed and disciplined and for whom I had strived in prayer). Thank you, God.

Part One

FOUNDATIONS
FOR BIBLICAL
CHILDREARING

Chapter

1

GETTING TO THE HEART OF BEHAVIOR

T HE SCRIPTURE TEACHES that the heart is the control center for life. A person's life is a reflection of his heart. Proverbs 4:23 states it like this: "Above all else, guard your heart, for it is the wellspring of life."

The word picture here is graphic. The heart is a well from which all the issues of life gush forth. This theme is restated elsewhere in the Bible. The behavior a person exhibits is an expression of the overflow of the heart.

You could picture it like this. The heart determines behavior. What you say and do expresses the orientation of your heart. Mark 7:21 states: ". . . from within, out of men's hearts, come evil thoughts, sexual immorality, theft, murder, adultery, greed, malice, deceit, lewdness, envy, slander, arrogance and folly." These evils in action and speech come from within—from the heart.

3

What your children say and do is a reflection of what is in their hearts.

Luke 6:45 corroborates this point:

> *The good man brings good things out of the good stored up in his heart, and the evil man brings evil things out of the evil stored up in his heart. For out of the overflow of his heart his mouth speaks.*

These passages are instructive for the task of childrearing. They teach that behavior is not the basic issue. The basic issue is always what is going on in the heart. Remember, the heart is the control center of life.

Parents often get sidetracked with behavior. If your goal in discipline is changed behavior, it is easy to understand why this happens. The thing that alerts you to your child's need for correction is his behavior. Behavior irritates and thus calls attention to itself. Behavior becomes your focus. You think you have corrected when you have changed unacceptable behavior to behavior that you sanction and appreciate.

"What is the problem?" you ask. The problem is this: Your child's needs are far more profound than his aberrant behavior. Remember, his behavior does not just spring forth uncaused. His behavior—the things he says and does—reflects his heart. If you are to really help him, you must be concerned with the attitudes of heart that drive his behavior.

A change in behavior that does not stem from a change in heart is not commendable; it is *condemnable*. Is it not the hypocrisy that Jesus condemned in the Pharisees? In Matthew 15, Jesus denounces the Pharisees who have honored him with their lips while their hearts were far from him. Jesus censures them as people who wash the outside of the cup while the inside is still unclean. Yet this is what we often do in childrearing. We demand changed behavior and never address the heart that drives the behavior.

What must you do in correction and discipline? You must require proper behavior. God's law demands that. You cannot, however,

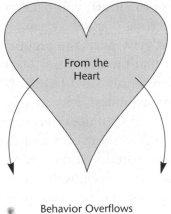

Behavior Overflows
(what we say and do)

Figure 1 The Heart Determines Behavior

be satisfied to leave the matter there. You must help your child ask the questions that will expose that attitude of the heart that has resulted in wrong behavior. How did his heart stray to produce this behavior? In what characteristic ways has his inability or refusal to know, trust, and obey God resulted in actions and speech that are wrong?

Let's take a familiar example from any home where there are two or more children. The children are playing and a fight breaks out over a particular toy. The classic response is "Who had it first?" This response misses heart issues. "Who had it first?" is an issue of justice. Justice operates in the favor of the child who was the quicker draw in getting the toy. If we look at this situation in terms of the heart, the issues change.

Now you have two offenders. Both children are displaying a hardness of heart toward the other. Both are being selfish. Both children are saying, "I don't care about you or your happiness. I am only concerned about myself. I want this toy. My happiness depends on possessing it. I will have it and be happy regardless of what that means to you."

In terms of issues of the heart, you have two sinning children. Two children are preferring themselves before the other. Two children are breaking God's law. Sure, the circumstances are different. One is taking the toy that the other has. The other is keeping the advantage. The circumstances are different, but the heart issue is the same—"I want my happiness, even at your expense."

You see, then, how heart attitudes direct behavior. This is always true. All behavior is linked to attitudes of the heart. Therefore, discipline must address attitudes of the heart.

This understanding does marvelous things for discipline. It makes the heart the issue, not just the behavior. It focuses correction on deeper things than changed behavior. The profoundest issue is what happens in the heart. Your concern is to unmask your child's sin, helping him to understand how it reflects a heart that has strayed. That leads to the cross of Christ. It underscores the need for a Savior. It provides opportunities to show the glories of God who sent his Son to change hearts and free people enslaved to sin.

This emphasis is the fundamental tenet of this book: The heart is the wellspring of life. Therefore, parenting is concerned with shepherding the heart. You must learn to work from the behavior you see, back to the heart, exposing heart issues for your children. In short, you must learn to engage them, not just reprove them. Help them see the ways that they are trying to slake their souls' thirst with that which cannot satisfy. You must help your kids gain a clear focus on the cross of Christ.

This proposition will inform everything you do as parents. It will dictate your goals. It will inform your methods. It will shape your model of how children develop.

This book will address all the facets of childrearing. We will look at a biblical view of the parenting task. We will examine child development. We will focus on parenting goals. We will think through training methods. In all these topics the core issue will be shepherding the heart.

I am not offering simple, clever methodology here. I am not promoting a new three-step plan for trouble-free children. I am not presenting a simple way to meet their needs so you can get on with your life. I am, however, willing to explore with you fresh ways of pursuing the training task God has given you. I offer these things as one who is not new to the task, but who hasn't grown cynical about parenting. I am more excited about this job than ever. I am full of hope and certain that God can enable us to raise from our homes a holy seed for the church.

I have seen families get hold of the principles in this book. I have seen parents shepherding happy, productive children who are alert to themselves and life. I visited such a home recently. The family was alive and vibrant. Teenage children were at home, because home was an exciting place to be. Father and Mother were held in high esteem and sought out for advice. The Bible and biblical truth blew through every conversation—not with stifling heat, but like a refreshing, life-giving breeze. In this home, five generations have kept the faith and a sixth is learning that God is the fountain of life in whose light we see light.

These are things worth striving for. This is a vision worthy of sacrifice.

If you are to sort through the welter of confusion about childrearing, you must go to the Scriptures for answers. I am committed to the fact that the Scriptures are robust enough to provide us with all the categories and concepts we need for this task. For too long the church has tried to integrate biblical and nonbiblical thought forms to answer the questions of parenting. The resulting synthesis has produced bitter fruit. We need to understand our task biblically.

You need to understand your child in relationship to the two broad sets of issues that affect him:

1) The child and his relationship to the shaping influences of life.
2) The child and his relationship to God.

In the next two chapters we will discuss these two arenas of child development.

——————— *Application Questions for Chapter 1* ———————

1. Explain the importance of dealing with the heart in discipline and correction of children.

2. Describe the centrality of the heart in directing behavior.

3. Why is it so easy to get sidetracked with behavior when issues of the heart are clearly so much more important?

4. What is wrong with a change in behavior without a change in the heart?

5. If the point of discipline is to direct the heart, how does that change the approach to discipline and correction?

2

YOUR CHILD'S DEVELOPMENT: SHAPING INFLUENCES

MY 11-YEAR-OLD SON was raising pigs and he was frustrated. The pigs overturned their water containers with their snouts, making it impossible to keep fresh water before them. We decided to make a concrete watering trough that would be too heavy to upset. We built a form of wood and began pouring concrete into the form.

As we worked, I began telling my boys how their young lives were like this project. The structures of our home were like the form. Their lives were the poured concrete. One day when the form was removed, they would be strong and useful. The disciplines of childhood would harden into concrete, adult lives. I waxed eloquent. They listened politely and appropriately. When I paused for a breath, they ran off to play, clearly unimpressed with the likeness between their young lives and swine troughs.

The boys were not ready that day for such heady thinking. I couldn't blame them. It is no easy matter to think through the influences that shape your children's lives. They are being shaped and molded by life's circumstances. All the aspects of family living have a profound impact on the persons your children become.

Shaping Influences

In this chapter, I will present a chart to help you understand the shaping influences of childhood. While the term "shaping influences" may be a new one, what it signifies is as old as humanity. Shaping influences are those events and circumstances in a child's developmental years that prove to be catalysts for making him the person he is. But the shaping is not automatic; the ways he responds to these events and circumstances determine the effect they have upon him.

There is clear biblical warrant for acknowledging the lifelong implications of early childhood experience. The major passages dealing with family (Deuteronomy 6, Ephesians 6, and Colossians 3) presuppose these implications. The Scriptures demand your attention to shaping influences.

The person your child becomes is a product of two things. The first is his life experience. The second is how he interacts with that experience. The first chart deals with the shaping influences of life. In the next chapter, I will introduce a chart addressing the child's response to those shaping influences. He is not merely acted upon by the circumstances of life. He reacts. He responds according to the Godward orientation of his heart. Understanding these charts will help you to know where your children need structure and shepherding.

The arrows in the diagram below represent these shaping influences. These influences, both within and outside parental control, come to the child and powerfully affect his life.

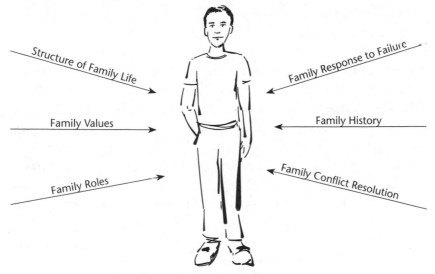

Figure 2 Shaping Influences

Structure of Family Life

One arrow depicts the structure of family life. Is the family a traditional nuclear family? How many parents is the child exposed to? Is it a family of two generations or three? Are both parents alive and functioning in the home? How are the parenting roles structured? Are there other children or is family life organized around only one child? What is the birth order of the children? What are the relationships between the children? How close or distant are they in terms of age, ability, interest or personality? How does the child's personality blend with the other members of the family?

Sally and her husband came for counseling. They were newly married and facing difficult adjustments. One of the hardest hurdles for Sally to surmount was that her husband did not organize his life around her. She'd been an only child. While her parents didn't spoil her by lavishing things on her, they did make her wants and needs a priority. She now felt unloved because her husband did not structure life around her wishes. Her family life as a child had profoundly shaped her needs and her expectations of her husband.

Family Values

Another arrow denotes family values. What is important to the parents? What is worth a fuss and what passes without notice? Are people more important than things? Do parents get more stressed over a hole in the school pants or a fight between schoolmates? What philosophies and ideas has the child heard? Are children to be seen and not heard in this home? What are the spoken and unspoken rules of family life? Where does God fit into family life? Is life organized around knowing and loving God or is the family in a different orbit than that? "See to it that no one takes you captive through hollow and deceptive philosophy, which depends on human tradition and the basic principles of this world rather than on Christ" (Colossians 2:8). The question you must ask is this: Are the values of your home based on human tradition and the basic principles of this world or on Christ?

I recently asked a young lad of ten what would get him into the most trouble, breaking a valuable vase or disobeying his parents' clear directive. Without a moment of hesitation, he said it would be far worse to break a cherished vase. This lad has learned the values of the home. He perceives an unspoken value that says prized vases are of greater concern to his parents than disobedient boys. These values are based on hollow and deceptive philosophies.

There are other aspects of family values. What are the boundaries within the family? Where are the secrets kept and when are they told? Are relationships with neighbors instinctively open or closed? How high are the walls around the family? Where can those walls be penetrated? Some families would never tell their relatives their problems but would freely disclose everything to a neighbor. Others would call a brother for help, but never a neighbor who is nearby (unlike the counsel in Proverbs 27:10). Some children grow up never knowing how much money Dad earns, while others know the checkbook balance on any given day. Some parents keep secrets from their children. Some children share secrets but not with their parents. Sometimes Mother and the children have secrets from Dad. Sometimes Dad and the children have secrets from Mom. Every family has established family boundaries. They may not be spoken or thought through, but they exist.

Family Roles

Within the family structure there are roles that each family member plays. Some fathers are involved in every aspect of family life. Others are busy and distanced from family activities. Subtle things like who pays the bills or who makes family appointments say much about family roles. Children have roles within the family, too. I know one home in which the children are required to put their father's socks and shoes on him because he is obese and finds it uncomfortable. By the cruel and harsh way he requires this service, he makes powerful shaping statements about their place in family life.

Family Conflict Resolution

Anyone who does marriage counseling can testify to the power of family influence in the resolution of problems. Does the family know how to talk about its problems? Do family members resolve things or do they simply walk away? Are problems solved by biblical principle or by power? Do the members of the family use nonverbal signals, like a dozen roses, to resolve conflicts? Proverbs 12:15–16 says: "The way of a fool seems right to him, but a wise man listens to advice. A fool shows his annoyance at once, but a prudent man overlooks an insult." A child is trained to be a fool or a prudent, wise man by the shaping influences of the home.

Sammy would get mad and run from the kindergarten class whenever he did not like what was going on. The teacher called his parents in for a conference. Sammy's dad got frustrated with the conference and abruptly left the room. The teacher gained a better understanding of why Sammy behaved this way.

Family Response to Failure

A related shaping issue is how the parents deal with their children's failures. Childhood is filled with awkward attempts and failed efforts. Immature children learning to master the skills of living in a sophisticated world inevitably make mistakes.

The important issue for our purposes is how those failures are treated. Are these children made to feel foolish? Are they mocked for their failures? Does the family find amusement at the expense of family members? Some parents show a marvelous ability to see failed attempts as praiseworthy efforts. They always encourage. They are adept at neutralizing the effects of a fiasco. Whether the child has known credible commendation or carping criticism or the mix of those things will be a powerful shaping influence in his life.

Family History

Another issue is each family's own history. Family members are born and others die. There are marriages and divorces. Families experience social stability or instability. There is enough money or not enough. Some enjoy good health while others must structure their lives around sickness or disease. Some have deep roots in the neighborhood, while others are uprooted continually.

I recently spent time helping a woman sort through the events of her childhood. Our conversation went like this:

Q: How many times did you move during childhood?
A: A lot of times.
Q: Five or ten?
A: Oh, no, more than that!
Q: Not more than twenty? [Here she stopped for a few minutes thinking and calculating.]
A: Many more than twenty.

She later told me that she and her sister had counted forty-six moves before age eighteen.

To be sure, that family history profoundly shaped this woman's values and perspectives.

This brief list is only suggestive of circumstances that have impact on our lives. The effect of these things on us is undeniable.

Mistakes in Understanding Shaping Influences

Two mistakes are made in interacting with the shaping influences of life. The first is seeing shaping influences deterministically. It is the error of assuming that the child is a helpless victim of the circumstances in which he was raised. The second mistake is denial. It is the mistake of saying the child is unaffected by his early childhood experience. Passages such as Proverbs 29:21 illustrate the importance of childhood experience. Here we see that the servant pampered from youth is affected in a manner that brings grief in the end.

Neither denial nor determinism is correct. You need to understand these shaping influences biblically. Such understanding will aid you in your task as parents.

You make a grave mistake if you conclude that childrearing is nothing more than providing the best possible shaping influences for your children. Many Christian parents adopt this "Christian determinism." They figure that if they can protect and shelter him well enough, if they can always be positive with him, if they can send him to Christian schools or if they can home school, if they can provide the best possible childhood experience, then their child will turn out okay.

These parents are sure that a proper environment will produce a proper child. They respond almost as if the child were inert. Such a posture is simply determinism dressed in Christian clothes.

I have a friend who is a potter. He told me that he can only create the type of pot the clay he is working with will allow him to create. The clay is not merely passive in his hands. The clay responds to him. Some clay is elastic and supple. Some clay is crumbly and hard to shape.

His observation provides a good analogy: You must be concerned with providing the most stable shaping influences, but you may never suppose that you are merely molding passive clay. The clay responds to shaping; it either accepts or rejects molding.

Children are never passive receivers of shaping. Rather, they are active responders.

Your son or daughter responds according to the Godward focus of his or her life. If your child knows and loves God, if your child has embraced the fact that knowing God can enable him to know peace in any circumstance, then he will respond constructively to your shaping efforts. If your child does not know and love God, but tries to satisfy his soul's thirst by drinking from a "cistern that cannot hold water . . ." (Jeremiah 2:13), your child may rebel against your best efforts. You must do all that God has called you to do but the outcome is more complex than whether you have done the right things in the right way. Your children are responsible for the way they respond to your parenting.

Determinism makes parents conclude that good shaping influences will automatically produce good children. This often bears bitter fruit later in life. Parents who have an unruly and troublesome teenager or young adult conclude that the problem is the shaping influences they provided. They think if they had made a little better home, things would have turned out okay. They forget that the child is never determined solely by the shaping influences of life. Remember that Proverbs 4:23 instructs you that the heart is the fountain from which life flows. Your child's heart determines how he responds to your parenting.

Mr. and Mrs. Everett had a rebellious 15-year-old son. They could see that they had made many mistakes in childrearing. Their mistakes, however, blinded them to his needs. When they saw their son, they saw their failures. As a result, they never saw him as a boy who was choosing to sin. They failed to see that he was choosing not to believe and obey God. They had not been perfect parents, it was true. Their son, however, had not been a good son. That part was true too.

Their view failed to consider the fact that human beings are creatures who are directed by the orientation of their hearts. The child is not inert during childhood. Your children interact with life. This leads us to our next chapter and our next chart.

Application Questions for Chapter 2

1. What have been some of the prominent shaping influences of your child's life?

2. What is the structure of your family? How has that affected your son or daughter?

3. What would your children identify as the values of your family? What are the things that matter most to you?

4. Where are the secrets in your home? Do you share too much and thus burden your children with problems too big for them? Do you share too little and thus insulate them from life and dependence on God?

5. Who is the boss in your home? Is there a centralized authority, or does your family make decisions by committee?

6. What are the patterns for conflict resolution? How have these patterns affected each of your children? Is change warranted? If so, what change?

7. What constitutes success or failure in your home?

8. What events have been pivotal in your family history? How have these events affected you? How have they affected your children?

9. Do you tend to be a determinist in the way you look at childrearing? Are you able to see that your children are active responders to the shaping influences in their lives? How do you see them responding?

3

YOUR CHILD'S DEVELOPMENT: GODWARD ORIENTATION

AS A COLLEGE STUDENT, I received my first exposure to sailing. I recall my amazement to learn that the direction of the craft is not determined by the direction of the breeze, but by the trim of the sail. In a sense, Godward orientation is like the set of the sail in a child's life. Whatever the shaping influences of life, it is the child's Godward orientation that determines his response to those shaping influences.

Proverbs 9:7–10 contrasts the mocker's and the wise man's responses to rebuke and instruction: "Whoever corrects a mocker invites insult; whoever rebukes a wicked man incurs abuse. Do not rebuke a mocker or he will hate you; rebuke a wise man and he will love you. Instruct a wise man and he will be wiser still; teach a righteous man and he will add to his learning. The fear of the LORD is the beginning of wisdom, and knowledge of the Holy One is understanding." Verse 10 helps us see what ultimately determines whether a child responds as a mocker or a wise man. It is the fear of the Lord that makes one wise and it is that wisdom that determines how he responds to the correction.

Godward Orientation

The figure below represents the child as a covenantal being. I use that expression to remind us that all human beings have a Godward orientation. Everyone is essentially religious. Children are worshipers. Either they worship Jehovah or idols. They are never neutral. Your children filter the experiences of life through a religious grid.

Romans 1:18–19 says: "The wrath of God is being revealed from heaven against all the godlessness and wickedness of men who suppress the truth by their wickedness, since what may be known about God is plain to them, because God has made it plain to them." All people have God's clear revelation of truth, but wicked people suppress that truth. They refuse to acknowledge and submit to the things God has made plain. Paul goes on to say that although they know God they do not glorify him, but become futile in their thinking and eventually worship idols.

In the language of Romans 1, your children either respond to God by faith or they suppress the truth in unrighteousness. If they

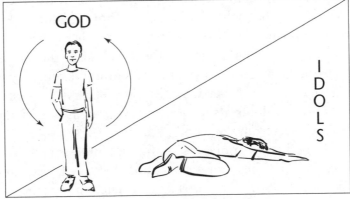

Figure 3 Godward Orientation

respond to God by faith, they find fulfillment in knowing and serving God. If they suppress the truth in unrighteousness, they will ultimately worship and serve the creation rather than the Creator. This is the sense in which I use the term "Godward orientation."

Choosing Between Two Ways

The upper left segment of the chart shows a person who is a worshiper of the one true God. The arrow pointing from God represents God, who is good and kind and holy. He has made all things for his glory. It is he under whose initiating and sustaining kindness all creatures dwell. To know him is to know life. The arrow pointing toward God indicates the Godward orientation of the heart. The person responds to God's goodness and kindness with love, delight, and worship. He wants to know and serve God better. The lower right division shows one who has exchanged the truth for a lie and is worshiping and serving created things rather than the Creator. He is involved in idolatry. He bows before things that are not God and that cannot satisfy.

To be sure, the young child may not be conscious of his religious commitment, but he is never neutral. Made in the image of God, he is designed with a worship orientation. Even as a young child, he is either worshiping and serving God or idols.

David reminds us of this in Psalm 58:3: "Even from birth the wicked go astray; from the womb they are wayward and speak lies." The words of Psalm 51:5 are even more familiar: "Surely I was sinful at birth, sinful from the time my mother conceived me." These verses are very instructive. Even a child in the womb and coming from the womb is wayward and sinful. We often are taught that man becomes a sinner when he sins. The Bible teaches that man sins because he is a sinner. Your children are never morally neutral, not even from the womb.

One of the justifications for spanking children is that "Folly is bound up in the heart of a child, but the rod of discipline will drive it far from him" (Proverbs 22:15). The point of the proverb is that something is wrong in the heart of the child that requires correction. The remedy is not solely changing the structure of the home; it is addressing the heart.

The Heart Is Not Neutral

Since there is no such thing as a place of childhood neutrality, your children either worship God or idols. These idols are not small wooden or stone statuary. They are the subtle idols of the heart. The Bible describes such idols using terminology such as fear of man, evil desires, lusts, and pride. The idols include conformity to the world, embracing earthly mindsets, and "setting the affections on things below." What we have in view are any manner of motives, desires, wants, goals, hopes, and expectations that rule the heart of a child. Remember, these things do not have to be articulated to be present.

As your children interact with their childhood experience, they interact based on their Godward orientation. Either they respond to life as children of faith who know, love, and serve Jehovah, or they respond as children of foolishness, and unbelief, who neither know him nor serve him. The point is this: They do respond. They are not neutral. They are not simply the sum total of what you and I put into them; They interact with life either out of a true covenant of faith or out of an idolatrous covenant of unbelief.

Whom Will the Child Worship?

It is imperative to be clear on this issue. Parenting is not just providing good input. It is not just creating a constructive home atmosphere and positive interaction between a child and his parent. There is another dimension. The child is interacting with the living God. He is either worshiping and serving and growing in understanding of the implications of who God is, or he is seeking to make sense of life without a relationship with God.

If he is living as a fool who says in his heart there is no God, he doesn't cease to be a worshiper—he simply worships what is not God. Part of the parent's task is to shepherd him as a creature who worships, pointing him to the One who alone is worthy of his worship. The question is not "will he worship?" It is always "whom will he worship?"

Implications for Childrearing

This issue of Godward orientation separates what you read here from most other books on childrearing. Most parenting books are written to help you do the best possible job of providing constructive shaping influences for your child. All sorts of tips and creative ideas are suggested for producing the best, most biblically consistent shaping influences, in the hope that the child will respond to things well and turn out okay. I am not only setting forth some ideas about biblical structures for life, but also approaches to shepherding the child by reaching his heart.

Remember Proverbs 4:23. Life flows out of the heart. Parenting cannot be concerned only with positive shaping influences; it must shepherd the heart. Life gushes forth from the heart.

I am interested in helping parents engage in hand-to-hand combat on the world's smallest battlefield, the child's heart. You need to engage your children as creatures made in the image of God. They can find fulfillment and happiness only as they know and serve the living God.

The task you undertake in childrearing is always concerned with both issues depicted in these charts. You want to provide the best possible shaping influences for your children. You want the structure of your home to furnish the stability and security that they need. You want the quality of relationships in your home to reflect the grace of God and the mercy for failing sinners that God's character demonstrates. You want the punishments meted out to be appropriate and to reflect a holy God's view of sin. You want the values of your home to be scripturally informed. You want to control the flow of events so that your home is not chaotic, but well-structured. You want to provide a healthy, constructive atmosphere for your child.

When all is said and done, those things, important as they are, will never be the total story. Your child is not just a product of those shaping influences. He interacts with all these things. He interacts according to the nature of the covenantal choices he is making. Either he responds to the goodness and mercy of God in faith or he responds in unbelief. Either he grows to love and trust the living God, or he turns more fully to various forms of idolatry and self-reliance. The story is not just the nature of the shaping influences of his life, but how he has responded to God in the context of those shaping influences.

Since it is the Godward orientation of your child's heart that determines his response to life, you may never conclude that his problems are simply a lack of maturity. Selfishness is not outgrown. Rebellion against authority is not outgrown. These things are not outgrown because they are not reflective of immaturity but rather of the idolatry of your child's heart.

Young Albert was a deceitful child. He sneaked around behind his father's back. He lied even when it was not advantageous. Often he would steal money from his parents. His father insisted on interpreting his behavior as immaturity. Albert was immature, but that was not the reason he was untrustworthy. The reason he could not be trusted was that he was a sinner. Al was trying to make sense out of life without God. In the idolatry of his rebellion against God's authority and his determination to be his own authority, he had become untrustworthy. Albert's dad was unable to help his son until he began to see that Al's behavior reflected a heart that had defected from God.

The Importance of Godward Orientation

Biblical stories show that shaping influences are not the whole story. Think of Joseph. His childhood experience was far from ideal. His mother died while he was young. He was his father's favorite. His dreams inflamed his brothers' hatred. He was further alienated from them by his father's gift of a coat that set him apart as their authority. His brothers betrayed him. He was thrown into a pit. Opportunistic slave traders bought him to profit from his resale value. He was double-crossed in Potiphar's house despite his honor and integrity.

He was imprisoned. Even there he was forsaken by those whom he had helped. Here was a man you would expect to be bitter, cynical, resentful, and angry. If man is only the sum total of influences that shape him, that would have been the result. Instead, what do we find? When his brothers threw themselves on the ground, begging for mercy, Joseph said to them, "'Don't be afraid. Am I in the place of God? You intended to harm me, but God intended it for good to accomplish what is now being done, the saving of many lives. So then, don't be afraid. I will provide for you and your children.' And he reassured them and spoke kindly to them" (Genesis 50:19–21).

How do we explain Joseph? He had a lens through which he viewed all the events of life. In the midst of difficult shaping influences, he entrusted himself to God. God made him a man who responded out of a living relationship with God. He loved God and found his orientation not in the shaping influences of his life but in the unfailing love and covenant mercies of God.

What about the servant girl to Naaman's wife? Enemy soldiers ripped her from her home in Israel and made her a house girl to an Aramean soldier. She was part of the plunder of war. The shaping influences in her life were far from ideal, yet she was faithful to Jehovah. When her master needed healing, this young girl knew God's power, and what is more, she knew where the prophet was in Israel. The King of Israel did not know the prophet or have deep faith in the power of God. He responded to the emergency with fear and unbelief (see 2 Kings 5:6–7). Why did this girl respond differently? Clearly, there is more to the person than shaping influences. Here is a girl who was given faith in Jehovah and retained it in spite of the difficult circumstances in which she was reared.

Summary

This is the point. There are two issues that feed into the persons your children become: 1) the shaping influences of life, and 2) their Godward orientation. Therefore, your parenting must be addressed to both of these issues. You must be concerned about how you structure the shaping influences of life that are under your control (many things are not, e.g. death, and so forth). Secondly, you must be actively shepherding the Godward orientation of your children. In all of this you must pray that God will work in and around your efforts and the responses of your children to make them people who know and honor God.

Figures 2 and 3 will provide direction and orientation as you seek to understand your task as parents. While you are concerned with biblical shaping influences, you must also shepherd the hearts of your children in the direction of knowing and serving God.

In the next chapter we will examine the foundational issues of parenting. What does it mean for the parent to function as God's agent? What is the nature of your task? What is the function of discipline and correction?

Application Questions for Chapter 3

1. Do you tend to be a determinist in the way you look at childrearing? Are you able to see that your children are active responders to the shaping influences in their lives? How do you see them responding?

2. What do you think is the Godward orientation of your children? Are their lives and responses organized around God as a Father, Shepherd, Lord, Sovereign, and King? Or do you see them living for some sort of pleasure, approval, acceptance, or some other false god?

3. How can you design winsome and attractive ways of challenging the idolatry you may see within your child?

4. How can you make your focus in correction the deeper issues of Godward orientation? How can you help your child see how he is investing himself in things that cannot satisfy?

5. Are you and your spouse spending time in prayer for God to reveal himself to your children? Ultimately, God initiates any work in your children's hearts.

You're in Charge

HE BOYS WERE OUT in the shed working on the go-cart. Our daughter went out to call them for dinner.

"You both are to go inside, wash up and get ready for dinner. Right now!" she announced authoritatively.

"Are the boys coming in?" my wife inquired, when our daughter had returned to the house alone.

"I called them," she said, with a look that betrayed her attempt to pull a power play on the boys.

Why hadn't the boys come in? Because it was their sister who had called them and they were not about to obey based on her authority.

She returned to the shed with the same message and added two powerful words, "Mother said. . . ."

Our daughter did not have the authority to order the boys into the house. The second time she called the boys, she called them as the agent of their mother. They knew it was time to come.

Confusion about Authority

Our culture does not like authority. It is not just that we don't like to be under authority, we don't like being authorities. One of the places where this is most clearly seen is in our discomfort with authority in the home.

We need a biblical understanding of authority. Questions abound. What is the nature of the parent's authority over a child? Is it absolute or relative? Is the authority vested in the parent because of the relative size difference between parents and young children? Are we in charge because we are smarter and more experienced? Are we called to rule because we are not sinners and they are? Do we have the right to tell our kids to do anything we want them to do?

If you don't answer questions such as these, you will be tentative and insecure in discharging your duty to God and to your children. If you are unsure about the nature and extent of your authority, your children will suffer greatly. They will never know what to expect from you because the ground rules will be constantly changing. They will never learn the absolutes and principles of God's Word that alone teach wisdom.

The culture in which you live does not have a biblical understanding of authority. We think of authority as derived either from overwhelming force or consent. Therefore, the only way we can respond is either with rebellion or servility. Our culture has no notion of intelligent, thinking persons willingly placing themselves under authority. When we allow our children to become independent decision makers we give them a false idea of liberty and a mistaken notion about freedom. Freedom is not found in autonomy, it is found in obedience. (Psalm 119:44-45).

Parents in our culture often improvise because they do not understand the biblical mandate to shepherd children. Parenting goals are often no more noble than immediate comfort and convenience. When parents require obedience because they feel under pressure, obedience of children is reduced to parental convenience.

Christian parents must clearly understand the nature of godly parenting and children must be trained that God calls them to obey always.

Called to Be in Charge

As a parent, you have authority because God calls you to be an authority in your child's life. You have the authority to act on behalf of God. As a father or mother, you do not exercise rule over your jurisdiction, but over God's. You act at his command. You discharge a duty that he has given. You may not try to shape the lives of your children as pleases you, but as pleases him.

All you do in your task as parents must be done from this point of view. You must undertake all your instruction, your care and nurture, your correction and discipline, because God has called you to. You act with the conviction that he has charged you to act on his behalf. In Genesis 18:19, Jehovah says, "I have chosen him [Abraham], so that he will direct his children and his household after him to keep the way of the LORD by doing what is right and just . . ." Abraham is on God's errand. He is performing a task on God's agenda. God has called him to these things. He is not freelancing. Abraham does not write his own job description. God defines the task and Abraham acts in God's behalf.

Deuteronomy 6 underscores this view of parental responsibility. In verse 2, God says his goal is for the Israelites and their children and grandchildren to fear the Lord by keeping his decrees. The person by whom God's decrees are passed on is the parent whom God calls to train his children when they sit at home, when they walk by the road, when they lie down, and when they rise up. God has an objective. He wants one generation to follow another in his ways. God accomplishes this objective through the agency of parental instruction.

Ephesians 6:4 commands you to bring your children up in the training and instruction of the Lord. This is a command to provide the training and instruction of the Lord; to function on God's behalf.

Understanding this simple principle enables you to think clearly about your task. If you are God's agent in this task of providing essential training and instruction in the Lord, then you, too, are a person under authority. You and your child are in the same boat. You are both under God's authority. You have differing roles, but the same Master.

If you allow unholy anger to muddy the correction process, you are wrong. You need to ask for forgiveness. Your right to discipline your children is tied to what God has called you to do, not to your own agenda.

Unholy anger—anger over the fact that you are not getting what you want from your child—will muddy the waters of discipline. Anger that your child is not doing what you want frames discipline as a problem between parent and child, not as a problem between the child and God. It is God who is not being obeyed when you are disobeyed. It is God who is not being honored when you are not honored. The issue is not an interpersonal contest, it is rather your insistence that your child obey God, because obeying God is good and right.

We know that there is such a thing as righteous indignation, but righteous indignation responds to an affront to God rather than an affront to us. It is easy for a parent to say, "I am right and I am angry, therefore my anger is righteous anger." It may be that we are just angry because we are not getting what we want.

Called to Obedience

You do not come to your child demanding, for your own purposes, that he knuckle under you and obey. No! You come with the corrections of discipline that are the way to life (Proverbs 6:23). You engage your son on behalf of God because God has first engaged you.

I recall many conversations that went like this:

FATHER: You didn't obey Daddy, did you?
CHILD: No.

FATHER: Do you remember what God says Daddy must do if
you disobey?

CHILD: Spank me?

FATHER: That's right. I must spank you. If I don't, then I would
be disobeying God. You and I would both be wrong.
That would not be good for you or for me, would it?

CHILD: No. [a reluctant reply]

What is this dialog communicating to the child? You are not spanking him because you are mean. You are not trying to force him to submit to you only because you hate insolence. You are not mad at him. You, like him, are under God's rule and authority. God has called you to a task you cannot shirk or shrug off. You are acting under God's rule. You are requiring obedience because God says you must.

Confidence to Act

There is tremendous freedom here for a parent. When you direct, correct, or discipline, you are not acting out of your own will; you are acting on behalf of God. You don't have to wonder if it is okay for you to be in charge. You certainly do not need your child's permission. God has given you a duty to perform; therefore the endorsement of your child is not necessary.

A Mandate to Act

Understanding that you are God's agent as a parent deals not only with the right to act—it also provides the mandate to act. You have no choice. You must engage your children. You are acting in obedience to God. It is your duty.

To illustrate, the state of Pennsylvania, where I live, requires schools to report any case of suspected child abuse. This law does not simply provide the right to report abuse. It requires that abuse be reported. The school official has no discretionary right to decide whether to report child abuse. The law requires it. In the same way, the fact that you are called by God to be an authority in the training of your children not only gives you the right, but also the responsibility, to train.

As a school administrator, I observe that most parents do not understand the appropriateness and necessity of being in charge in their child's life. Rather, parents take the role of adviser. Few are willing to say, for instance, "I have prepared oatmeal for your breakfast. It is a good, nutritious food and I want you to eat it. Maybe other mornings we will have something you like better." Many are saying, "What do you want for breakfast? You don't want the oatmeal I have prepared; would you like something else?" This sounds very nice and enlightened, but what is really happening? The child is learning that he is the decision maker. The parent only suggests the options.

This scenario is repeated in the experience of young children in clothing choices, schedule choices, free-time choices and so forth. By the time the child is six or eight or ten, he is his own boss. By age thirteen the child is out of control. Parents can cajole, plead, urge (in frustration and anger), scream and threaten, but the child is his own boss. The parent has long since given up the decision-making prerogative in the child's life. How did it happen? It crept in at a very early age as the parent made every decision a smorgasbord of choices for the child to decide.

Some may argue, "Children only learn to be decision makers as parents allow them to make decisions. We want children to learn to make sound decisions." This misses the most important issue. Children will be good decision makers as they observe faithful parents modeling and instructing wise direction and decision making on their behalf.

Preliminary even to decision making is the importance for children to be under authority. Teach your children that God loves them so much that he gave them parents to be kind authorities to teach and lead them. Children learn to be wise decision makers by learning from you.

Parents must be willing to be in charge. You should do this with a benevolent and gracious manner, but you must be an authority for your children.

Parenting Defined

Recognizing that God has called you to function as his agent defines your task as a parent. Our culture has reduced parenting to providing care. Parents often see the task in these narrow terms. The child must have food, clothes, a bed, and some quality time.

In sharp contrast to such a weak view, God has called you to a more profound task than being only a care-provider. You shepherd your child in God's behalf. The task God has given you is not one that can be conveniently scheduled. It is a pervasive task. Training and shepherding are going on whenever you are with your children. Whether waking, walking, talking or resting, you must be involved in helping your child to understand life, himself, and his needs from a biblical perspective (Deuteronomy 6:6–7).

If you are going to shepherd your children, you must understand what makes your children tick. If you are going to direct them in the ways of the Lord, as Genesis 18 calls you to, you must know them and their inclinations. This task requires more than simply providing adequate food, clothing and shelter.

Clear Objectives

It is instructive to ask parents what concrete training objectives they have for their children. Most parents cannot quickly generate a list of the strengths and weaknesses of their children. Nor can they articulate what they are doing to strengthen their child's weak areas or to encourage his strengths. Many moms and dads have not sat down and discussed their short-term and long-term goals for their children. They have not developed strategies for parenting. They do not know what God says about children and his requirements for them. Little thought has been given to methods and approaches that would focus correction upon attitudes of heart rather than merely on behavior. Sadly, most correction occurs as a by-product of children being an embarrassment or an irritation.

Why is this? Our idea of parenting does not include shepherding. Our culture sees a parent as an adult care-provider. Quality time is considered having fun together. Fun together is not a bad idea, but it is light years away from directing your child in the ways of God.

In contrast to this, Genesis 18 calls fathers to direct their children to keep the way of the Lord by doing what is right and just. Being a parent means working in God's behalf to provide direction for your children. Directors are in charge. It involves knowing and helping them to understand God's standard for children's behavior. It means teaching them that they are sinners by nature. It includes pointing them to the mercy and grace of God shown in Christ's life and death for sinners.

Humility in Your Task

Understanding that you function as God's agents can keep you sharply focused and humble as parents. It is sobering to realize that you correct your child by God's command. You stand before him as God's agent to show him his sin. Just as an ambassador is conscious of functioning in behalf of the country that has sent him, so the parent must be aware of the fact that he is God's representative to the child. I know of no realization that will sober and humble the parent like this one.

On many occasions, I have had to seek the forgiveness of my children for my anger or sinful response. I have had to say, "Son, I sinned against you. I spoke in unholy anger. I said things I should not have said. I was wrong. God has given me a sacred task, and I have brought my unholy anger into this sacred mission. Please forgive me."

Your focus can be sharpened by the realization that discipline is not you working on your agenda, venting your wrath toward your children; it is you coming as God's representative, bringing the reproofs of life to your son or your daughter. You only muddy the waters when the bottom line in discipline is your displeasure over their behavior, rather than God's displeasure with rebellion against his ordained authority.

No Place for Anger

I have spoken to countless parents who genuinely thought their unholy anger had a legitimate place in correction and discipline. They reasoned that they could bring their children to a sober fear of disobeying if they showed anger. So discipline became the time when Mom or Dad manipulated their children through raw displays of anger. What the child learns is the fear of man, not the fear of God.

James 1 demonstrates the falsehood of the idea that parents should underscore correction with personal rage:

> *My dear brothers, take note of this: Everyone should be quick to listen, slow to speak and slow to become angry, for man's anger does not bring about the righteous life that God desires.*
> (James 1:19–20)

The Apostle James could not be more clear. The righteous life that God desires is never the product of uncontrolled anger. Unholy human anger may teach your children to fear you. They may even behave better, but it will not bring about biblical righteousness.

Any change in behavior that is produced by such anger is not going to move your children toward God. It moves them away from God. It moves them in the direction of the idolatry of fearing man. No wonder James adds emphasis by saying, "Dear brothers, take note of this. . . ."

If you correct and discipline your children because God mandates it, then you need not clutter up the task with your anger. Correction is not displaying your anger at their offenses; it is rather reminding them that their sinful behavior offends God. It is bringing his censure of sin to these subjects of his realm. He is the King. They must obey.

Benefits to the Child

The parent comes to the child in God's name and on God's behalf. As parents, you can teach your child to receive correction from you because it is the means God has appointed. The child learns to receive correction, not because parents are always right, but because God says the rod of correction imparts wisdom, and whoever heeds correction shows prudence (Proverbs 15:5, 29:15).

The child who accepts these truths will learn to accept correction. I have been humbled and amazed to see my children, in their late teens and early twenties, accept correction, not because I brought it to them in the best possible manner, but because they were persuaded that "He who ignores discipline despises himself, but whoever heeds correction gains understanding" (Proverbs 15:32). They understand that their dad is God's agent, used by God in the role of authority to direct in God's ways. Therefore, even though I am not a flawless instrument of God's work, they know that receiving correction will bring them understanding.

Summary

Discerning these issues can give you strength and courage as you do the job to which God has called you. You are the authority over your child, because God has called you to direct (Genesis 18:19). You provide direction under God's authority. Your right to be in charge is derived from God's authority. You need not be tentative or overbearing. You are God's agent to teach his ways to your child. You are God's agent to help your child understand himself as a creature in God's world. You are God's agent to show the need for God's grace and forgiveness. You look to God to give you strength and wisdom for your task.

Clear thinking about the function of discipline illustrates the importance of seeing yourself as God's agent, called by God to be in charge.

Discipline: Corrective, Not Punitive

If correction orbits around the parent who has been offended, then the focus will be venting anger or, perhaps, taking vengeance. The function is punitive. If, however, correction orbits around God as the one offended, then the focus is restoration. The function is remedial. It is designed to move a child who has disobeyed God back to the path of obedience. It is corrective.

Discipline: An Expression of Love

Making small talk during a coffee break at a pastor's conference, I overheard someone else's conversation. Two fathers were talking about their children and I couldn't resist listening in.

"I'm too hard on them," commented Dad #1. "I discipline them all the time. I really have to; my wife loves them too much to discipline them."

"I guess you and your wife need to strike some sort of a balance," Dad #2 observed.

"Yes," continued Dad #1 reflectively. "We need some balance between discipline and love."

I almost choked on my doughnut! Balance discipline and love? I thought of Proverbs 3:12: ". . . the LORD disciplines those he loves, as a father the son he delights in." Proverbs 13:24 rushed to mind: "He who spares the rod hates his son, but he who loves him is careful to discipline him." Revelation 3:19: "Those whom I love, I rebuke and discipline." How can you balance discipline and love? Discipline is an expression of love.

The conversation that I overheard is not uncommon. Many parents lack a biblical view of discipline. They tend to think of discipline as revenge—getting even with the children for what they did. Hebrews 12 makes it clear that discipline is not punitive, but corrective. Hebrews 12 calls discipline a word of encouragement that addresses sons. It says discipline is a sign of God's identification with us as our Father. God disciplines us for our good that we might share in his holiness. It says that while discipline is not pleasant, but painful, it yields a harvest of righteousness and peace.

Rather than being something to balance love, it is the deepest expression of love.

God provides the understanding of what discipline is. Its function is not primarily punitive. It is corrective. The primary thrust of discipline is not to take revenge, but to correct. The discipline of a child is a parent refusing to be a willing party to his child's death (Proverbs 19:18).

What makes this idea so hard to get hold of? It is difficult because of what we discussed above. We don't see ourselves as God's agents. We, therefore, correct our children when they irritate us. When their behavior doesn't irritate us, we don't correct them. Thus, our correction is not us rescuing our children from the path of danger; it is rather us airing our frustration. It is us saying to them, "I am fed up with you. You are making me mad. I am going to hit you, or yell at you, or make you sit on a chair in isolation from the family until you figure out what you did wrong."

What I have just described is not discipline. It is punishment. It is ungodly child abuse. Rather than yielding a harvest of righteousness and peace, this sort of treatment leaves children sullen and angry. Is it any wonder that children resist the will of someone who moves against them because they have been an irritation?

Discipline as positive instruction rather than negative punishment does not rule out consequences or outcomes of behavior. Consequences and outcomes of behavior are certainly part of the process God uses to chasten his people. The Bible illustrates the power of proper outcomes to show blessing on obedience and the destruction that comes with sin and disobedience. We will look at this more later.

While it is true that disciplined children are a joy to their parents (Proverbs 23:15–16, 24), as God's agents you cannot discipline for mere matters of self-interest or personal convenience. Your correction must be tied to the principles and absolutes of the Word of God. The issues of discipline are issues of character development and honoring God. It is God's non-negotiable standard that fuels correction and discipline.

Your objective in discipline is to move toward your children, not against them. You move toward them with the reproofs and entreaties of life. Discipline has a corrective objective. It is therapeutic, not penal. It is designed to produce growth, not pain.

There are other parenting issues with which to be concerned. You must understand more than what it means to function as God's agent. You must be concerned with more than the nature of discipline. Parents must be goal-directed. In the next chapter we will explore the issue of parenting goals. What are biblical goals for parenting? What things have we adopted from our culture that we must assess and address?

—————— *Application Questions for Chapter 4* ——————

1. What do you think is the nature of your authority as a parent? How does this square with a biblical view?

2. How frequently does your correction of your children boil down to an interpersonal contest rather than an underscoring of God's authority over your children?

3. What are some things you can do to keep your discipline focused on turning your children to the paths of life?

4. How do you present your authority to your children? Do you ever find yourself saying things like "I am your father/mother, and as long as you live here, you're going to have to listen to me!"?

5. How would you describe your job as God's agent for discipline? How will seeing yourself as God's agent change the way you discipline?

6. Would you be willing to sit down and analyze the following for your children: training objectives, list of your child's strengths and weaknesses, short-term and long-term goals, and strategies for parenting?

5

EXAMINING
YOUR GOALS

$\mathcal{I}$T WAS A COOL, brisk fall day. In spite of the light rainfall, it was a festive—a vintage western Pennsylvania—homecoming day. The band played. Every group, from the Future Farmers of America to the Veterans of Foreign Wars, marched along the parade route. We were chilly beneath our umbrella, but who could walk away from all this homey entertainment? At the end of the parade was a troupe of junior majorettes ages three to five. One near the rear caught my eye. She looked to be under three years of age. Her skimpy costume left her body exposed to the elements. She was crying. As the troupe marched in the drizzle she kept breaking rank—running to her mother. There was no comfort there. Her mother kept pushing her back to her place in the rank. I will never forget the sense of desperation and confusion in the eyes of this tyke as she marched by us sobbing.

This mother's actions implied certain parenting goals. We may suppose that she wanted her daughter to be beautiful and sought-after. She knew that you can't start too young to prepare

your child to fulfill your childhood dreams. This was important
to Mom. It doesn't require too much imagination to fill in Mom's
agenda, or to imagine how this girl spent her childhood.

I do not know the mother in question. I am not sure of her specific
goals or how self-conscious she was of the things that drove her to
make sacrifices, to run alongside the troupe, bent over, urging her
child to hold the baton correctly and keep in line. I *am* sure of this:
She had goals for her daughter. We all have. There are objectives
that direct our choices as we raise our children. Some folks can
articulate their goals. Other goals may be implied by the choices
parents make.

Unbiblical Goals

Parents want children to be successful so they can "do well" and
live happy, comfortable lives. This wish for success has a different
shape and definition for different people, but every parent wants
successful, happy children. We want them to have adult lives filled
with opportunity and unfettered by problems. However we define
success, we wish it for our children. We are well aware that their
upbringing has much to do with future success.

There are scores of ways parents try to produce this success.
Helping parents produce successful children is a growth industry.
Books purporting to show the way to success are legion. Programs
are developed and marketed. Experts in psychology, theology, education, athletics, and motivation have exhausted themselves and
their audience. Let's look at several ways parents can prepare their
children to be successful.

Developing Special Skills

Some parents involve their children in a broad range of activities.
They hustle them to baseball, football, hockey, soccer, gymnastics,
swimming, dance class, and piano lessons. These skills are not evil
and may have their place in your children's lives. But is the measure

of the parent the number of activities provided for the child? Is the measure of the child the number of skills developed?

Even if this frenetic pace of activity could be proved beneficial, have you no concern as a Christian parent for the values implied and taught by the coaches and instructors of these activities?

Will involvement in these activities have biblical content? Will your children receive biblical instruction in an accurate self-image, sportsmanship, loyalty, poise, endurance, perseverance, friendship, integrity, rights, competition, and respect for authority?

Clearly, you must understand what success is. Will true success depend on the skills which these activities teach? What is a biblical definition of success?

Psychological Adjustment

Other parents strive for more psychological goals. Driven by vivid recollection of their own childhood, they are preoccupied with Billy's and Suzie's psychological adjustment. Books and magazines pander to these parents. They promote the latest pop psychology—all tailored to insecure moms and dads. These gurus promise to teach you how to build self-esteem in your children. Have you noticed that no books promise to help produce children who esteem others?

How can you teach your children to function in God's kingdom, where it is the servant who leads, if you teach them how to make the people in their world serve them?

Some child psychologists, appealing to your own sense of being used, offer strategies for teaching your offspring to be effective with people (manipulation made easy). Still other experts, pandering to your fear of overindulging your children, promise children who are not spoiled. Every issue of the book-of-the-month club catalog has its pop-psychology-for-children offerings. Parents buy them by the millions, bowing to the experts who tell them what kind of training their children need. This is the question you must ask: Are these psychological goals for Christians? What passages of Scripture direct you to these goals?

Saved Children

I have met many parents whose preoccupation is getting their children saved. They focus on getting their child to pray "the sinner's prayer." They want him to ask Jesus to come into his heart. They take Johnny to Child Evangelism Fellowship functions, Good News Clubs, summer camps or anywhere else where someone will bring him to a decision to trust Christ.

They think that if their child would get saved, all the problems of living would be solved. Sometimes parents feel this way because, in their own experience, getting saved was a spiritual watershed. They want their child to have that experience too.

This is a sensitive issue that must be tempered by two facts: 1) You can never know with absolute certainty whether your child is saved. Many passages such as the "Lord, Lord" passage at the end of the Sermon on the Mount (Matthew 7:21–23) indicate that false faith can carry someone a long way. The heart can even deceive itself. Thus, the Bible warns about the dangers of being self-deceived and exhorts you to test yourself to see whether you are in the faith. 2) A child's profession of faith in Christ does not change the basic issues of childrearing. The parent's goals are the same. The things the child is called to are the same. He requires the same training he required before. He will have times of tenderness and times of spiritual coldness. The parent's task does not change when the child makes a decision.

There are many passages that teach the need to shepherd, to train, to instruct, and to discipline your children. None of these passages has getting a child to pray the "sinner's prayer" as its focus.

Family Worship

Some parents are persuaded that the family that prays together stays together, so they determine to have daily Bible reading times. Each family member must be present. They are conscientious about the need for daily devotions. But, as valuable as family worship is, it is no substitute for true spirituality.

I know a family that never missed family worship. They read the Bible and prayed each day. But in family living and family values there was no connection between the family worship routine and life.

While family worship is valuable, the family worship of the family described above reflected a defective spirituality.

Well Behaved Children

Some succumb to the pressure to raise well behaved kids. We help them develop poise. We teach them to converse. We want children who possess social graces. We want them to be able to make guests comfortable. We want them to be able to respond with grace under pressure. We know that these skills are necessary to be successful in our world. It pleases us to see these social graces in our children.

I'm a pastor who has raised three children. I'm certainly not down on well behaved children. Yet, having well behaved children is not a worthy goal. It is a great secondary benefit of biblical childrearing, but an unworthy goal in itself.

You cannot respond to your children to please someone else. The temptations to do so are numerous. Every parent has faced the pressure to correct a son or daughter because others deemed it appropriate. Perhaps you were with a group when Junior did or said something that you understood and were comfortable with, but that was unquestionably misread by others in the room. Stabbed by their daggers of disapproval, you felt the need to correct him for the sake of others. If you acquiesce, your parenting focus becomes behavior. This obscures dealing biblically with Junior's heart. The burning issue becomes what others think rather than what God thinks. Patient, godly correction is precluded by the urgent pressure to change behavior. If your goal is well behaved kids, you are open to hundreds of temptations to expediency.

What happens to the child who is trained to do all the appropriate things? When being well-mannered is severed from biblical roots in servanthood, manners becomes a classy tool of manipulation. Your children learn how to work others in a subtle but profoundly self-serving way. Some children become crass manipulators of others and disdainful of people with less polish. Others, seeing through the sham and hypocrisy, become brash and crass rejecters of the conventions of culture. In the late 1960s and early 1970s, scores of young adults rejected etiquette in an attempt to be real and un-pretending. Either reaction is a casualty of manners detached from the biblical moorings of being a servant.

Good Education

In my years as a school administrator, I have met scores of parents whose goal for their children was a good education. These parents are driven. They will work with Suzie for hours each night. They coach and prod, they encourage and warn, they will stop at nothing to have their child succeed. Their goal is seeing their child achieve academic awards and scholarly recognition. They are persuaded that education brings success. Unfortunately, scores of disillusioned and broken people are thoroughly educated. It is possible to be well-educated and still not understand life.

Control

Some parents have no noble goal at all; they simply want to control their children. These parents want their children to mind, to behave, to be good, to be nice. They remind their children of how things were when they were youngsters. Frequently they employ the "tried and true" methods of discipline—whatever their parents did that seemed to work. They want children who are manageable. They want them to do the right thing (whatever that is at the mo-ment). The bottom line is to control their kids. But the control is not directed toward specific character development objectives. The concern is personal convenience and public appearance.

The Biblical Warning Against Cultural Influence

Any student of the Old Testament knows that God was concerned about Israel's susceptibility to influence from the people of Canaan. He commanded Israel to drive the nations out, to show no mercy.

God knew that if the people of Canaan lived alongside Israel, they would go astray.

Like Old Testament Israel, you too, are subject to the powerful influence of your culture. Like Israel, you must reject things in the culture that are abhorrent to Jehovah your God.

It is one thing to be painfully aware of unbiblical objectives such as these we have sketched. It is another thing to embrace scriptural objectives. There are so many areas in which children require direction. What goal is broad enough and flexible enough to be suitable to all stages of child development?

What general biblical objectives will guide and focus your view of life and therefore your training of your children? What is a worthy biblical goal? The familiar first question of the *Shorter Catechism* answers these questions.

Q. What is the chief end of man?
A. Man's chief end is to glorify God and to enjoy him forever.

Is there any other goal that is worthy? Are you willing to start here with your children? You must equip your children to function in a culture that has abandoned the knowledge of God. If you teach them to use their abilities, aptitudes, talents, and intelligence to make their lives better, without reference to God, you turn them away from God. If your objectives are anything other than "Man's chief end is to glorify God and enjoy him forever," you teach your children to function in the culture on its terms.

How do we do this? We pander to their desires and wishes. We teach them to find their soul's delight in going places and doing things. We attempt to satisfy their lust for excitement. We fill their young lives with distractions from God. We give them material things and take delight in their delight in possessions. Then we hope that somewhere down the line they will see that a life worth living is found only in knowing and serving God.

In terms of Godward orientation, we are training them in the idolatry of materialism. In fact, we even feed the idols. Years spent denying the importance of a deep conviction of scriptural truth will not develop into godly piety during adolescence or early adulthood.

No wonder we lose our kids. We lose them because we fail to think clearly about man's chief end. The chief end of man is to glorify God and enjoy him forever; therefore, your objective in every context must be to set a biblical worldview before your children. From their earliest days, they must be taught that they are creatures made in the image of God—made for God. They must learn that they will only "find themselves" as they find him. Your child must grow to see that real living is experienced when he stands before God and says, "Whom have I in heaven but you? And earth has nothing I desire besides you" (Psalm 73:25). If this is what you want for your children, then you must ensure that the content of everyday life fits this objective.

Mixed Signals

Psalm 36 asserts that it is only in his light that we see light. We, however, present a different world to our children. In our attempt to help them adapt to a culture that does not know God, we present objectives to pursue and ways of solving life's problems that are unbiblical. In effect, we train them to think unbiblically. These unbiblical patterns of thought and habits of action are at cross purposes with life lived for the glory of God.

For example, if you teach your child to obey and to perform for approval from you and from others, you present an unbiblical objective. God says we should do all for his glory, because his eye is upon us and he is the rewarder of the just. People will respond well to a child who obeys, but you cannot make that secondary benefit of obedience the primary reason for obeying.

Another example may be helpful. What advice do you give your child when she is confronted with abusive children on the school bus? Many parents would urge their child to fight fire with fire, to follow the return-evil-with-evil pattern. Some parents teach their child to ignore a bully. But is either advice biblical? Not really. God says to return good for evil, all the while entrusting ourselves to the protective care of a God who says, "It is mine to avenge; I will repay" (Romans 12:19).

Biblical counsel leads your children to entrust themselves to God's care and protection. It teaches sensitivity to the needs of the offender. "If your enemy is hungry, feed him" (Romans 12:20). It reminds her that God says to bless those who curse us. In short, it is counsel that can only function in the context of biblical revelation. This counsel directs the child to God and not to his own resources.

In the next chapter we will rethink these goals in light of the chief end of man.

Application Questions for Chapter 5

1. How do you define success? How would your child complete this sentence? "What Mom and Dad want for me is. . . ."

2. You are pushed and pulled by the things that are listed under unbiblical goals. Which of these unbiblical goals influences your parenting the most adversely?

3. Remember, you are a shaping influence for your children. What makes you tick? What would you say drives you day by day? What do you fear, love, feel anxious about? What are the values taught in your home?

4. Like Old Testament Israel, you are affected by the culture around you. How has the culture impacted your view of children and your goals for your children?

5. Are you in tune with the idea of living for the glory of God? Does that thought pulsate for you, or is it a bland religious idea?

6. What are the subtle ways you are tempted to teach your children to function in society on its terms?

7. What mixed signals do you send to your children? Examples:

1. Doing your best is all that matters to me. / I don't want to see any more C's on your report card.

2. Life does not consist in the abundance of possessions. / Wait till you see what I got for you!

8. True spiritual shepherding is a matter of nurture, not just energy spent getting your children saved. How will this affect what you do with them?

9. Are the spoken and unspoken rules of your family life consistent with true spirituality—living for the glory of God?

6

REWORKING
YOUR GOALS

$\mathcal{T}$HE FIRST STEP in building a house is excavation. The excavator's job is site preparation. He pushes away the brush, dead trees, and unwanted stumps to prepare a place to build. Our last chapter was site preparation; we have cleared the brush. Now we are ready to build on the site.

Rethinking Unbiblical Goals

If the goals in the last chapter are unworthy, let's rethink our goals in light of the chief end of man—to glorify God and enjoy him forever. Bear in mind, in this discussion, that the issue here is not whether these goals are lawful or beneficial for Christians to pursue. The issue is whether they are adequate as ultimate goals.

Developing Special Skills

What is the problem with having your children involved in a broad range of activities? Many parents who would never allow their children to attend public school will send them to dance classes. They will refuse to have them influenced by secular humanism in school, but will expose them to unbiblical ideas of beauty in dance class.

When I ask parents why they put their children in these classes, they explain that it has helped their child's sense of self-worth. Are there any passages that make the development of self-worth a biblically mandated goal? Shouldn't we be more concerned with an accurate sense of self? Is it biblical to build self-worth on a child's capacity to develop a physical skill? Are we not encouraging pride that comes from the capacity to perform? Most coaches do not teach the Little Leaguer who hits a home run to give thanks to God for the timing and coordination necessary to perform such a complex feat.

Many of these activities teach your children to trust in themselves, when the Scripture says that those who trust in themselves are fools whose hearts turn from God. The self-love and self-trust our culture proffers always turns the heart away from God.

What values do you teach by the sacrifices needed to practice each day? Many families who always have time for team practice are unable to organize family life around regular times of family Bible reading and prayer. What values are taught? What values are taught when the Lord's Day worship plays second fiddle to baseball practice or a swim meet? All this because children need to build their self-esteem!

A biblical worldview dictates that you should teach your children to exercise and care for their bodies as an expression of stewardship for God's gifts. Abilities should be developed because God has given the stewardship of talents and special capacities. Skills that would make your children more able to serve and open channels of ministry to others should be encouraged.

Athletic activities can be a valuable way of providing family unity and oneness. Rather than fracturing families by allowing each to go his own way for fitness, such activities can serve to teach family loyalty in sharing each other's interests in games and play.

Strenuous activity is valid to keep the body in excellent health. You must be concerned with strength and stamina for a life of service to God. Activities that provide flexibility, strength and cardiovascular health are necessary for usefulness in God's kingdom.

Our family found that a 650-mile bicycle-camping trip provided physical, mental, and spiritual challenge that was easily focused on biblical goals. Our son, Tedd, quickly realized that love of family dictated a change in his riding technique. If the cycle tour was to be a family affair, he could not keep a cadence that would put him too far ahead of less-skilled riders. His desire to serve kept the sport from becoming sport for sport's sake.

Psychological Adjustment

What about concern for psychological adjustment? Let's think through a social example. What do you do in response to the bully? Many parents want to help their child learn the "manly art of self-defense." They try to teach their sons how and when to fight. I have heard Christian parents give their sons this advice: "Don't you ever start a fight, but if someone starts a fight with you, then you end it." In other words, "Don't be the aggressor, but if need be, knock his block off." Biblical advice? How can a parent get from "knock his block off" to "pray for God's help"? Shall we pray for God's help to knock his block off?

In a biblical vision, you should instruct your children to entrust themselves to God in the face of unfair treatment. You should teach them the principles of the Scripture. Romans 12:17–21 tells us that the only weapon strong enough to overcome evil is good. We are exhorted to leave vengeance with God. He will deal with the issue of justice. Luke 6:27–36 helps us understand how to love our enemies and do good to those who hate us. It promises that we will be sons of the One who is kind to ungrateful and wicked people. 1 Peter 2:23 tells us to face injustice without retaliation, entrusting ourselves to God. You should encourage your children to see the needs of those around them. You should help them learn to make peace. You should teach that a soft answer turns away wrath. Train your children to use occasions when hurt to learn how to love God and deepen their trust and confidence in him.

Saved Children

Let's rethink this matter of getting your children saved. Perhaps one of the problems with this perspective is that it looks for a major spiritual event of salvation and misses the spiritual process of nurturing your children. It is our task to faithfully teach our children the ways of God. It is the Holy Spirit's task to work through the Word of God to change their hearts. Even when the Spirit illuminates and quickens them to life, it is a life of progressive growth.

What your children need is spiritual nurture. They need to be taught the ways of God. They need to be instructed in the character of God so that they can learn a proper fear of God. They need to understand that all of life rushes toward the day when we shall stand before God and give account. They need to learn about the pervasive effects of the fall on the human condition. They need to understand subtleties of the malignancy of their own hearts. They need to know the dangers of trusting in themselves. They need answers to the great problems of life. They need to understand the difference between presuppositional thinking and empiricism. In short, they need nurturing instruction.

Nurture them. Tenderly encourage them to trust God. They need to trust him not only for salvation, but for daily living. Teach them how knowing God impacts on the experience of being bullied in the school yard. This will make a difference in how they interact with their failures and successes. Knowing God will make a difference when they are afraid, angry, hurting, sinning, or sinned against. Knowing what God is like will speak to them when they are tempted. Knowing God will affect the long-term goals for their lives. You must help your children understand the rich treasures of living in the vitality of a robust and lively faith in Jesus.

You must always hold out to your children both their need of Christ's invasive redemptive work and their obligation to repent of their sin and place their faith in Jesus Christ. Repentance and faith are not rites of initiation to Christianity. Repentance and faith are the way to relate to God. Repentance and faith are not acts performed one time to become a Christian. They are attitudes of the heart toward ourselves and our sin. Faith is not just the way to get saved; it is the lifeline of Christian living.

Your children must understand what it means to repent, not just "of all my sins" in some generalized way, but of specific sins of heart idolatry. They need to know the cleansing and refreshing forgiveness of God, not just once to get saved, but daily. They must understand the Christian life not simply as living according to a biblical code, but as life in faith, commitment, and fellowship with the living God.

Family Worship

Family worship must function in the broader, richer sense that I have described in the paragraphs above. It's easy to have a shift of means and end. The practice of family worship is a means, not an end. It is a means to the end of knowing God. The name of the game is not daily family worship per se; it is knowing God. The end is knowing God. A means to employ in reaching that end is family worship.

You need family worship that connects with your children and their lives. You must be creative and flexible in assuring that your family worship serves the shepherding and nurturing tasks we have outlined above.

Reading the Proverbs daily is of great benefit to children (and to adults). Our daily practice was to read one-third of a chapter of Proverbs before school each day. This was a rich source of wisdom and encouragement for our children. We have seen them learn and then later internalize the principles in this practical section of the Word of God. The Proverbs serve as an owner's manual for life. Proverbs confronts a child with every aspect of true spirituality.

When our children were little, we would read Old Testament passages and act them out. I have been Goliath (with the help of a chair). We have hidden in caves (under the table) with David as he ran from Saul. Reading some of the Psalms of persecution in that setting made them come alive for our children. One day, we packed our things and set out on foot, talking about Abraham who left Ur not knowing where he would go, only knowing God would go with him. We tried to imagine walking away from our home knowing we would never come back again. We tried to imagine not knowing where we would go.

Why do all this? For this simple reason: to make the Bible truth live for our children. Always remember that the goal of family worship is knowing God. When you lose sight of that goal, family worship becomes an empty ritual. You need only read Isaiah 1 to see how God feels about empty ritual.

Well Behaved Children

What about the earlier example of raising well behaved children? You cannot use Miss Manners' approach because it is simply an elaborate means of pleasant social manipulation. In a biblical vision, manners are an expression and application of the duty of loving my neighbor as myself. It is a matter of teaching children to imitate the Lord Jesus' self-giving as set forth in Philippians 2.

When saying "please" and "thank you" are rooted in what it means to look out for the interests of others, they become expressions of biblical love. Waiting to eat until all are served is not just an empty social convention; it is a way of showing consideration for those around you. Good behavior must be rooted in those rare qualities that the Apostle Paul saw in Timothy: "I have no one else like him, who takes a genuine interest in your welfare. For everyone looks out for his own interests, not those of Jesus Christ" (Philippians 2:20–21).

Good Education

What about academic goals? Parents typically pressure their children to get good grades. Are good grades a biblical objective? What scripture passages would support this objective? Then parents may add to the unbiblical objective some unbiblical incentives. "I'll pay you one dollar for every 'A' you get on a test." Or perhaps parents say, "If you work hard, you will be able to get a good job and earn lots of money when you grow up." A biblical objective? Hardly! Proverbs 23:4 says the opposite: "Do not wear yourself out to get rich."

I am not denying in any sense that those who are faithful will be richly rewarded. Of course that is true, but one cannot work simply for that reward as his goal.

In contrast, there should be no pressure for good grades at all. Grades are unimportant. Some children can achieve "A's" without any diligent effort. Others struggle for a good solid "C". What is important is that your child learn to do his work diligently for God. God has promised that he will reward the faithful. Knowing that gifts and abilities are a stewardship from the Lord, your child's objective should be faithfulness. You need to train your child to find in Christ the strength and power to work for God's glory. Anything else is training him to think and act unbiblically.

Objections Answered

I can hear my reader object, "What if my children are not believers?" We will address this later, but for the moment, do you suppose we should teach unbelievers to disobey the law of God? Is not God's standard applicable to all, regardless of whether they believe? Do we dare give the mechanisms and approaches that help them learn to manipulate their world without God? Such things will only drive them away from Christ.

If you faithfully hold out God's standard, you are keeping before them the Law of God that is a schoolmaster to take them to Christ. Faced with being kind to one who abuses you, there is nowhere to go but to God, who alone can enable a person to respond in love. When your child's heart desires revenge, when she must love an enemy, when her faith demands she leave room for God's justice—there is no place to go but to the cross. She will not be able to embrace these things without embracing Christ. Thus, you are always pointing to Christ and his work, power, and grace.

Getting help from Christ was powerfully illustrated in the life of our daughter. As a ninth grader she seemed to get on the wrong side of her Spanish teacher. Through four years of high school she struggled with feeling angry over being sinned against. We spent many hours talking about how to respond. We discussed the impossibility of her loving this lady apart from God's grace. We encouraged her to find hope, strength, consolation, and comfort in Christ. One day, when she was a senior, my wife observed a note in the margin of Heather's Bible making application of Romans 12 to her relationship with her Spanish teacher. She worked through the spiritual disciplines necessary to know Christ's help in this daily struggle.

Teaching your children to live for the glory of God must be your overarching objective. You must teach your children that for them, as for all of mankind, life is found in knowing and serving the true and living God. The only worthy goal for life is to glorify God and enjoy him forever.

If you accept this goal as the only one worthy of your attention and effort, what methods must you employ to help embrace this goal for living? We address those methods in the next chapter.

Application Questions for Chapter 6

These questions are the same ones we thought about at the end of chapter 5. How has your understanding of these issues been changed by the Word of God?

1. How do you define success? How would your child complete this sentence? "What Mom and Dad want for me is. . . ."

2. You are pushed and pulled by the things listed under unbiblical goals. Which of these unbiblical goals influences your parenting the most adversely?

3. Remember, you are a shaping influence for your children. What makes you tick? What would you say drives you day by day? What do you fear, love, feel anxious about? What are the values taught in your home?

4. Like Old Testament Israel, you are affected by the culture around you. How has the culture impacted your view of children and your goals for your children?

5. Are you in tune with the idea of living for the glory of God? Does that thought pulsate for you, or is it a bland religious idea?

6. What are the subtle ways you are tempted to teach your children to function in the society on its terms?

7. What mixed signals do you send to your children? Examples:

    1. Doing your best is all that matters to me. / I don't want to see any more C's on your report card.

    2. Life does not consist in the abundance of possessions. / Wait till you see what I got for you!

8. True spiritual shepherding is a matter of nurture, not just energy spent getting your children saved. How will this affect what you do with them?

9. Are the spoken and unspoken rules of your family life consistent with true spirituality—living for the glory of God?

DISCARDING UNBIBLICAL METHODS

A LITTLE GIRL CAUGHT my eye. She was a beautiful child. Every detail of her clothing and grooming spoke of wealth. She and her mother, like me, were waiting for a flight.

This child's beauty was external, for she was demanding and petulant. It was apparent that her mother, weary from traveling, was about to assert her authority.

The child whined on, demanding this and that, refusing to be pacified. Her mother tried to settle her. The child was implacable. Then it happened.

Exasperated, her mother finally turned on her. "I am sick of you," she said. "I hate you. Go away. Find someone else to yell at. I don't want you. I can't stand you. Get out of my sight," she gestured.

With that, she picked up her things and moved away from her daughter.

The little girl might have been able to hold out against this power play in normal circumstances, but here, in a strange airport, she felt frightened.

She moved toward her mother, "I'm sorry, Mommy. I love you, Mommy."

"Go away. I don't know you. . . ."

"I'm sorry, Mommy," this time in desperation.

"Go away. I hate you. . . ."

The airline called my flight. When I last saw them, the little girl was still pleading and the mother was lecturing and scolding.

Viewed from one perspective, some might say this is successful parenting. This mother was confronted with a demanding, unreasonable child. She was able within a few minutes to change her daughter's behavior. From another perspective, all would agree that the mother's method was wrong. While she was able to change her daughter's behavior, she did so at a powerful cost. The cure was worse than the disease.

We cannot be indifferent to methodology. Biblically, the method is as important as the objectives. God speaks to both issues. He is concerned not only with what we do, but also with how we do it.

Our culture does not provide us with biblical models. Here, as in the area of goals, we must identify and reject the non-biblical approaches that vie for our attention. Biblical goals require a biblical approach—only godly methodology will bring glory to God.

Unbiblical Methods

Unbiblical approaches come to us in many ways. Books and magazines regularly address childrearing. There is always a market for approaches that promise some hope of success. Talk-TV programs bring on experts. Sometimes we just fall back on the familiar patterns by which we were raised.

Various approaches have one thing in common: The human mind is the standard. It may be our own mind—"There is nothing wrong with what my father did. . . ." It may be the mind of others—"Dr. 'So & So' on talk-radio advocated this and it sounds good to me. . . ." Faith in the human mind as a sufficient reference point for itself is implicit in each of these examples.

Let's identify the prevalent methods.

I Didn't Turn Out So Bad

Sadly, many parents have not thought through methodology. They just get mad and yell. When they have "had it up to here," they threaten, holler, hit their kids and grow increasingly frustrated. Sometimes this is done in the name of biblical discipline. After all, they don't want to be permissive parents with undisciplined children. When challenged, they often respond like this: "My Dad yelled at me. He used to knock me around once in a while. I didn't like it, but I turned out okay."

What has this parent done? He has unquestioningly accepted and employed the same method of childrearing his parents used. He has not assessed whether it was biblical. He has not assessed whether it had a good impact on him. He has simply drawn from his survival the implication that it wasn't that bad.

In the example above, the "I didn't turn out so bad" method was confrontational and abusive. Other applications of this method may not involve confrontation and abuse. Perhaps parents were indulgent and permissive. Maybe they caved in and were easily manipulated. The point is that many parents unquestioningly employ whatever method their parents employed. When they correct their kids, they are simply echoing their parents' words and tones.

Pop Psychology

I recently heard a talk-radio guest discuss motivating children. His approach to the problem was bribery. In fact, he used the term bribery to identify his method. His counsel was to make deals. Use your power as the adult to make bribes that encourage the behavior you desire.

Your son won't clean his room. Bribe him. Each week he keeps his room clean, buy him a new Nintendo game, or give him $5. All you have to do is be creative enough to find a bribe that works with each of your children.

Another variety of this method is contracts. Make a contract with your daughter. Spell out an agreement that commits you to perform certain things if she performs certain things. Make contracts that ensure that the things that you want are done. (We quickly forget that the child's mind can circumvent any contract the parent's mind can conceive.)

These approaches are superficial. The point of appeal in bribery and contracts is crass self-interest. Bribery latches on to evil in the child's heart and uses it as a motivation. The child is not taught to look out for the interests of others. The child learns nothing about being under authority because God is God and the parent is his agent. The child does not learn biblical reasons for integrity, responsibility, or neatness in one's room.

These methods will not be satisfying to a parent who understands that the heart determines behavior. Such methods do not deal biblically with the heart. They are only concerned with instances of behavior. Unfortunately, the heart is being trained, but it is not trained in biblical motives or goals.

Behavior Modification

Some pop-psychology methods apply behavior modification. The idea is simple. Reward good behavior in some tangible way; ignore or perhaps punish bad behavior. While I am not against praising children for doing what is right, I reject the notion that children should be rewarded for fulfilling normal responsibilities.

Behavior-modification provides a reward for doing what is deemed good. Junior does well with a household chore and so he gets to go out for ice cream. If he fails to do some assigned task, he receives some privation. The hope is that the child will respond to the rewards and privations by becoming well behaved.

Since the heart and behavior are so closely linked, whatever modifies behavior inevitably trains the heart. The heart is trained to greedy self-interest and obtaining rewards. The point of appeal is to Junior's greed. Because Junior lives a lust-driven life in which he will perform for ice cream and other goodies, the program seems to work. But your methods inevitably instruct the heart—the heart determines behavior.

One family I know developed a very clever application of behaviorism. Each time their children responded to anything in a good way they put the child's name on a piece of paper and put it in a jar.

If the child brushed her teeth, helped with dishes, cleaned her room, set the table, or did anything commendable, her name went into the jar. If she did something wrong, her name came out of the jar. At the end of the week a name was drawn from the jar and the winning child got a present.

The children quickly learned the point of the game. Get your name in the jar as much as possible. The more times your name was in the jar, the greater your chance of winning.

You're wondering how it worked. It worked great. It was an effective tool for teaching the children. It taught them to be selfish. It taught them to do things for improper motives. It taught them how to earn parental approbation and therefore, a name in the jar. They quickly learned what would get their name in the jar and how to maximize the number of times for a minimum amount of effort. They became manipulators of the system. When Mother wasn't around to notice good behavior, there was no point in being good. The system effectively moved this family away from biblical action springing from biblical motives.

Let me note in passing that biblical incentives and rewards are not an end in themselves, but rather the outcomes of obedience to God. There is temporal blessing attached to obedience. The God who knows our hearts calls us to right behavior for the purpose of honoring him. He honors those who honor him (1 Samuel 2:30).

Emotionalism

Another method is emotionalism. This is what the mother in the opening illustration was using. She appealed to the child's fear of being left alone in a strange airport. The appeal was to her daughter's sense of emotional well-being. She knew her daughter could not deal with the emotional threat of being left alone in the airport.

Some use this same emotional approach in a "kinder" way. I have heard parents say, "It really makes me feel bad when you talk like that. You are hurting my feelings. . . ." Here, again, the point of reference is emotional well-being.

Another variety of emotional appeal is to shame a child. A young girl in my acquaintance is routinely shamed with threats about her actions spoiling her father's reputation as a community leader. The appeal is not to obey for the glory of God. Rather, it is an emotion-laden shaming for putting her father's credibility at risk by her unacceptable behavior.

A family in my acquaintance has systematically used another form of emotional privation. They reject a spanking as cruel. They place their misbehaving daughter in a chair alone in the middle of the living room for a specified period of time. As long as the child is being punished in the chair, no one in the family may speak to her or have any contact with her. She is isolated from the family, which carries on as if she were not even there. Asked what makes her sadder than anything, this 7-year-old girl replied, "I am saddest when I am on the chair, and my Daddy is home, but he won't talk to me."

This approach is not only cruel, but ineffective in addressing the heart biblically. This young girl is not learning to understand her behavior biblically. She is not learning to discern the specific issues of the heart that her behavior reflects. What she is learning is to avoid the emotional privation of being on the chair. Her heart is being trained, but not to know and love God. She is being trained to respond to the crippling fear of emotional privation.

While she is likely to become hardened to this method of discipline, we may expect it to have a long-term effect. She may be driven by a lifelong desire to please her parents and secure their approbation. Or she may internally distance herself from her parents in order to be insulated from further hurt. Whether she is compliant or rebellious, she is not learning to live out of a desire to know and serve God.

Punitive Correction

Some parents utilize a punitive approach. These parents use the threat of punishment to control their children. There are many variations on this theme. The punishment may be being hit or yelled at. The punishment may be simple privation of something that the child desires. The attempt is to keep the child under control through the negative experience of punishment. I am not decrying a biblical use of the rod, but rather an impulsive response of angry frustration.

Grounding is perhaps the most popular form of privation. Children are grounded from their bikes, the phone, from going outside, from the TV, from other children, or even other family members. As I write, I am aware of a 10-year-old who has been grounded to his room for several weeks. He may only leave his room to go to school, or to eat, or to go to the bathroom.

The problem here is that none of the issues that caused the poor behavior for which he is grounded are being addressed. I asked his folks what they thought grounding was doing for him. They looked at me with blank stares. You see, grounding is not designed to do something for the child; it is designed to do something against him.

Grounding is not corrective. It is simply punitive. It does not biblically address the issues of the heart that were reflected in the child's wrong behavior. It simply punishes for a specified period of time. Nothing my young friend needs to know is being learned. He is learning to cope with grounding, but his character flaws are not addressed. He is not learning to understand the deceitfulness of his heart. He is not learning God's ways. He is not being taken to Christ, who can enable a 10-year-old to know how to serve God.

I have often wondered why grounding is so universally popular. I believe it is because it is easy. It doesn't require ongoing interaction. It does not require ongoing discussion. It does not assess what is going on inside the child. It does not require patient instruction and entreaty.

Grounding is quick, incisive, simple. "You're grounded for a month. Go to your room."

Perhaps parents just don't know anything more constructive to do. They feel frustrated. They realize that something is wrong with their child. They don't know how to get to it. They feel they need to respond in some way.

One thing is for sure. Grounding does not address the issues of the heart in a biblical way. The heart is being addressed, but it is addressed wrongly. The child will learn to cope with the grounding, but may never learn the things that a godly parent desires for him to learn. My 10-year-old friend is rather philosophical about it.

"It's not too bad," he said to me, "I can play and watch TV in my room. If I don't let it bother me, it isn't that bad." He has learned to live under house arrest.

Erratic Eclecticism

This approach is exactly what the name implies. It is erratic in that it moves about. There is no consistency. It is eclectic as it freely draws from many sources. The parent gets bits and pieces from a variety of methods. A few ideas picked up skimming the *Reader's Digest* in the supermarket checkout are joined to ideas from a chat session in the church nursery. And so it goes. Like a rolling snowball picking up snow, ideas are added along the way.

For a few weeks, Mom and Dad try contracts. That gets boring and doesn't seem to work as well for them as it did for someone else. They hear a sermon about spanking and decide that is the need. Maybe they waited too long to start this. They try grounding for a spell. They try a season of emotional appeals. They use bribery for a few days. Mostly, they feel frustrated, scared, and yell a lot.

Their children are confused. They are not sure what Mom and Dad want. They are never sure what system is in effect now. In the end, they are worse off than if Mom and Dad had picked almost anything and stuck with it.

You could probably add to this brief list several other possible methods of childrearing. This list is only suggestive. We need a biblical methodology.

Evaluating Unbiblical Methods

Where do these unbiblical methods take us? What kind of fruit do they bear? While we have discussed several differing approaches, they all lead to the same problems. They lead to superficial parenting, rather than shepherding the hearts of our children. They only address behavior. Hence, they miss the point of biblical discipline.

Biblical discipline addresses behavior through addressing the heart. Remember, the heart determines behavior. If you address the heart biblically, the behavior will be impacted.

The expediency of dealing with behavior rather than the heart means that deep needs within the child are ignored. You can't respond to Suzie yelling at Jimmy by simply telling her to stop yelling. The problem is not that she is yelling at her brother. The problem is the anger and bitterness in her heart that her yelling expresses. If you only try to change behavior, you are missing the real issue—her heart. If you can successfully address the real issue, the behavior problem will be solved.

Superficial parenting that never addresses the heart biblically produces superficial children who do not understand what makes them tick. They must be trained to understand and interpret their behavior in terms of heart motivation. If they never have that training, they will drift through life, never understanding the internal struggles that lie beneath their most consistent behavior.

Parenting that focuses only on behavior does address the heart. The problem is that the heart is addressed wrongly. Changing behavior without changing the heart trains the heart toward whatever you use as your means. If it is reward, the heart is trained to respond to reward. If approbation, the heart is trained to strive for approval, or to fear disapproval. When the experts tell you that you must find what works with each child, they are saying you must find the idols of the heart that will move each child.

Your child is a covenantal creature. The heart is the well-spring of life. Addressing the child's heart unbiblically plays to the corruption of his heart as an idolater and provides him with functional idols around which to organize his life. In this sense, whatever you do addresses the heart. When I note above that the heart is not addressed, I mean it is not addressed biblically.

There is another problem. If you address only behavior in your children, you never get to the cross of Christ. It is impossible to get from preoccupation with behavior to the gospel. The gospel is not a message about doing new things. It is a message about being a new creature. It speaks to people as broken, fallen sinners who are in need of a new heart. God has given his Son to make us new creatures. God does open-heart surgery, not a face-lift. He produces change from the inside out. He rejects the man who fasts twice a week and accepts the sinner who cries for mercy.

Let's imagine you are dealing with the problem of a child's failure to do his homework. Here are several common, but unbiblical, approaches used to change a child's behavior.

Bribery approach: "Do your work all week and I'll take you to the ball game."

Emotional approach: "Please do your work. I get so upset when you don't. It makes me feel like crying. I wonder where I went wrong." Or, "I have invested an awful lot in your education and you are making me feel that I have wasted my money."

Punitive approach: "You didn't do your work, so no TV for a week. If you fail again tomorrow it will be no TV for two weeks. . . ."

Behavior modification approach: "For every day you do your work, I'll put a slip of paper in the jar with your name on it. . . ."

I-didn't-turn-out-so-bad approach: "If I didn't do my work, Grandpa used to smack me around. It didn't hurt me; I learned to do my work . . . (smack)." Or perhaps, "When I didn't do my work, he left me alone and sooner or later I learned my lesson. It's your problem, not mine."

What has each of these approaches accomplished? It is hoped that each has resulted in getting the kid to do his work. The question is this: How can you move from any of these approaches to the precious, life-giving truth that God sent his Son to set people free from sin? The above approaches don't lead to the message of the gospel. The heart is being trained away from Christ and his cross.

Character development is ignored. The emphasis is on getting homework done. Children are not being trained to make ethical choices as responsible people living in reverence for God. They are learning how to jump through your hoops and avoid your displeasure. They learn to make choices based on expediency rather than principle.

There is another devastating effect of this approach to discipline. It produces distance between parent and child. Children soon see through the implicit and explicit manipulation. They eventually come to resent the crass attempts to control their behavior. They learn to play the cat-and-mouse game with you, but depth of relationship and communication is lost. As they get older and can begin to imagine living independently of Mom and Dad, they become more resistant to the manipulation and perhaps even openly rebellious.

Even the apparent success stories in unbiblical parenting are deceiving. Perhaps you have seen your upbringing in these illustrations. You may be one of those who says, "I didn't turn out so bad." Perhaps you never openly rebelled against your folks. Maybe you are like a friend of mine. She went to college. She got her degree. She was married and has children. From a distance she doesn't seem that messed up, but she knows the internal struggles with self-doubt. She knows what it is to live with the fear of man. She craves approval. She was never taught to understand her behavior in terms of attitudes of heart. She has trouble getting from the problems in her life to Christ. The Christian life doesn't make sense to her. While she has never seen a counselor or appeared to others as being a basket case, she has been devastated by unbiblical parenting and the idolatrous interaction of her heart with those unbiblical approaches.

Remember, God is not only concerned with the "what" of parenting, he is concerned with the "how." The Bible speaks to the issues of methodology. What direction does the Bible give us for dealing with these issues? The next chapter addresses these questions.

─────── *Application Questions for Chapter 7* ───────

1. Have you thoroughly thought through what you are doing as a parent? Have you subjected the things you say and do in response to your child to biblical critique?

2. Which of the unbiblical methods above have you seen yourself use? Can you think of any other common unbiblical approaches to discipline and correction?

3. What is wrong with these unbiblical approaches? State it in your own terms.

4. How would you defend this statement: The behavior of our children is not the problem—the root issue is their hearts.

5. Could you label this figure and relate it to the central idea of this chapter?

6. Could you summarize the point of this chapter in a single sentence?

EMBRACING
BIBLICAL METHODS:
COMMUNICATION

ALESMEN TIRE OF restaurant food. My father understood this, so he would often bring salesmen home for dinner. During one such evening, when we were hesitant in obeying, Dad reminded us of our duty by asking, "What is Ephesians 6:1?" In our minds we would recite, "Children obey your parents in the Lord," and proceed with our task.

The powerful effect this question had on us impressed our guest. He was sure he had stumbled on a new method of getting children to obey. By evening's end he could contain his curiosity no longer.

"By the way," he finally asked, "What is Ephesians 6:1? I would like to teach it to my children."

Like many parents, my father's friend wanted an effective method of dealing with his children. He thought perhaps this Ephesians 6:1 approach would work with his kids.

If we reject the methods that we evaluated briefly in the last chapter, to what do we turn? What light does the Word of God shed on our approach to parenting? God's Word must inform not only our goals, but also our methods.

Methods and goals should be complementary. You want your child to live for the glory of God. You want your child to realize that life worth living is life lived under the Lordship of Jesus Christ. Your methods must show submission to that same Lord. Methods designed to produce well-adjusted and successful children won't work because your goal is not simply success and good adjustment.

A biblical approach to children involves two elements that you weave together. One element is rich, full communication. The other is the rod. In the book of Proverbs we find these two methods side by side.

> Do not withhold discipline from a child;
>   if you punish him with the rod,
>   he will not die.
> Punish him with the rod
>   and save his soul from death.
> My son, if your heart is wise,
>   then my heart will be glad;
>   my inmost being will rejoice
>   when your lips speak what is right.
> Do not let your heart envy sinners,
>   but always be zealous for the fear of the LORD.
> There is surely a future hope for you,
>   and your hope will not be cut off.
> Listen, my son, and be wise,
>   and keep your heart on the right path.
>   (Proverbs 23:13–19)

> Listen to your father, who gave you life,
>   and do not despise your mother when she is old.
>   (Proverbs 23:22)

> My son, give me your heart
>   and let your eyes keep to my ways. . . .
>   (Proverbs 23:26)

These passages couple the rod with rich entreaty. Solomon weds extensive communication and the rod. Both are essential to biblical childrearing. Together they form a God-pleasing, spiritually satisfying, cohesive, and unified approach to discipline, correction, and training of children. The use of the rod preserves biblically-rooted parental authority. God has given parents authority by calling them to act as his agents in childrearing. The emphasis on rich communication prohibits cold, tyrannical discipline. It provides a context for honest communication in which the child can be known and learn to know himself. It is sensitive, but avoids a "touchy-feely" sentimentality.

The rod and communication must always be woven together in the actual shepherding of children. In order to study each, we will separate them. We will first look at communication (chapters 8–10), and then the rod (chapter 11).

Here is an excerpt from a recent conversation I had with a father.

"Tell me about your communication with your son," I queried.

"Oh, we talk okay," he responded. "Just last night he told me he wanted a bicycle and I told him to eat his beans."

The comment brought a smile to my face, but as I reflected on it, I realized it was probably an accurate description of communication between most parents and their children. Moms and dads tell the children what to do. Kids tell their parents their wishes and dreams.

Communication is Dialogue, Not Monologue

We often think of communication as the ability to express ourselves. Accordingly, we think of ourselves as talking *to* our children. Instead, you should seek to talk *with* your children. Communication is not monologue. It is dialogue.

It is not only the ability to talk, but also the ability to listen. Proverbs 18:2 speaks to this issue with penetrating insight: "A fool finds no pleasure in understanding but delights in airing his own opinions." Proverbs 18:13 reminds us that "He who answers before listening—that is his folly and his shame."

The finest art of communication is not learning how to express your thoughts. It is learning how to draw out the thoughts of another. Your objective in communication must be to understand your child, not simply to have your child understand you. Many parents never learn these skills. They never discover how to help their children articulate their thoughts and feelings.

There is a certain irony in all this. When children are little, we often fail to engage them in significant conversation. When they try to engage us, we respond with uninterested "uh huh's." Eventually, they learn the ropes. They realize that we are not interested in what goes on in them. They learn that a "good talk" for us is a "good listen" for them. When they become teens, the tables turn. Parents wish they could engage their teens, but the teens have long since stopped trying.

Crystal is a good example. Her parents brought her for counseling. They said she was withdrawn. They knew she was in trouble, but she would not talk to them. Her mother was a screamer. Communication was limited to periods of volcanic activity. When Mom spewed forth lava, Crystal learned to head for cover. Her father was a withdrawn, distancing person. He rarely engaged anyone. Crystal, age fourteen, is boiling and surging inside, but has never had the benefit of her parents' understanding involvement. With biblical counseling she is learning to talk and Mom and Dad are learning how to draw her out and then listen to what she says.

Focus on Understanding

Your first objective in correction must not be to tell your children how you feel about what they have done or said. You must try to understand what is going on inside them. Since the Scripture says that it is out of the abundance of the heart that the mouth speaks, you must engage your children to understand what is going on inside.

What is important in correction is not venting your feelings, anger or hurt; it is, rather, understanding the nature of the struggle that your child is having. What is important is understanding the "why" of what has been done or said. You need to understand not just what has happened, but what is going on within your child. Remember, it is out of the abundance of the heart that the mouth speaks. Your question in correction is this: What is the specific content of the abundance of the heart in this circumstance? What was the temptation? What was his response to that temptation? What was he trying to accomplish? If you can understand and help your child understand these things, you will be on your way to understanding the "why" of what has transpired. What you must do is peel away the behavior and discern the inner world of your child's motivation in this situation. While you can never understand the issues of the heart flawlessly, it is a pursuit worthy of effort.

Imagine this scenario: Your child is putting on his new sneakers. You knew last night when you bought them that he was not really happy with them, but they were the only ones you could afford. Now, as he is getting ready for school, he is crying. How are you going to handle this one? If your objective is to let him know what you think, you may say something like this:

"Look, I know you don't like the sneakers, but that's all I could afford. Don't be such a baby. What would Jared say if I told him you were crying over something like this? They're just going to get messed up anyway. In a couple of days no one will know what they look like. What do you care about what those kids think about your sneakers? Who made them the experts anyhow? You should be thankful you even have them. Those sneakers you don't like cost more than my first car. Look, I have to go to work; I have more important things to worry about than sneakers. . . ."

Now, if your primary objective is to understand the child's internal struggles, you could have a conversation like this:

PARENT: You're upset about the sneakers, aren't you?
CHILD: Yeah.
PARENT: I didn't think you liked them when we bought them last night. You didn't want to tell me, did you?

CHILD: No.

PARENT: What don't you like about them?

CHILD: They look stupid.

PARENT: I don't know what you mean.

CHILD: Jared says they look stupid.

PARENT: When did Jared see them? We just got them last night.

CHILD: Chris got a pair just like this and Jared told everybody in class that he looked like a dweeb.

PARENT: What's a dweeb? Oh, never mind. What looks dweeby about those sneakers?

CHILD: This red stripe on the back. They don't put red stripes on the new ones. They're last year's shoes—that's why they were only $87.98.

PARENT: Oh, I see. You're afraid that they will call you a dweeb today, right?

CHILD: Yeah.

PARENT: That really hurts, doesn't it?

CHILD: Yeah. I don't know why they should care about what my shoes are like, but I know they'll call me a dweeb.

What are you learning? Your child is struggling with feelings that you can identify with. There is a genuine pressure out there in his third-grade classroom. He is feeling the pressure to be approved by his peers. This circumstance is bringing out the hopes and fears of his heart.

Your communication objective can be stated in several simple propositions.

1. The behavior you see is a reflection of the abundance of your child's heart.
2. You want to understand the specific content of the abundance of his heart.
3. The internal issues of the heart are of greater import than the specifics of behavior, since they drive behavior.

To summarize: You want to understand your child's inner struggles. You need to look at the world through his or her eyes. This will enable you to know what aspects of the life-giving message of the gospel are appropriate for this conversation.

If you are going to understand and help your child understand himself, there are skills you must develop. You must learn to help your children to express themselves. You must learn to facilitate conversation. You must know how to comprehend behavior and words. You must strive to discern matters of the heart. Proverbs 20:5 says, "The purposes of a man's heart are deep waters, but a man of understanding draws them out." As a parent, you want to be such a person of understanding.

Think about the Incarnation of Jesus Christ. It is a good model for interaction with your children. God could have remained off in heaven. He could have spoken through cloud and thunder as he did in Exodus 19. But what does God do in the incarnation? He comes to earth to dwell with us. He takes on flesh and blood like your flesh and blood. He takes a human psychology like we have. He accepts all the limitations of a man on the earth; he can only be in one place at one time. He experiences all the things we experience. He is tired and hungry at Jacob's well in John 4. He weeps at Lazarus' tomb. Hebrews 2 says "He suffered when he was tempted."

You see, in the Incarnation, God comes to dwell with us in such a way that he can look at the world through your eyes. He fully understands what it is to be human and to face the temptations that human beings experience. That is the triumphant note of Hebrews 4.

Therefore, since we have this great high priest who has passed through the heavens, Jesus the Son of God, let us hold firmly to the faith we possess. For we do not have a high priest who is unable to sympathize with our weaknesses, but we have one who has been tempted in every way, just as we are—yet was without sin. Let us then approach the throne of grace with confidence, so that we may receive mercy and find grace to help us in our time of need.

(Hebrews 4:14-16)

Jesus can look at the world through your eyes.

I would have to confess, to my shame, that often my children had a father who was unable to sympathize with their weaknesses. I was too focused on correcting external behavior and not focused enough on understanding my kids.

But, as it often was for me, dealing with disobedience is a wonderful opportunity to draw alongside our children. As you learn their internal struggles with sin, you have an inside track. You, like they, are a sinner. You can use your insight into the nature of temptation to help them understand their own battles. You can also encourage your children that the unending grace and mercy that you have found in Jesus Christ is offered to them as well. In him there is righteousness that we cannot produce, forgiveness that we cannot merit, and power that we cannot generate. There is hope for needy people in this one who became flesh and dwelt with us.

In which of the imaginary conversations above can the gospel be most powerfully presented? The answers are obvious. You will have to develop skill at probing the heart if you want to really understand your children. Most parents have had this sort of conversation with their children:

MOM: Why did you hit your sister?
JUNIOR: [pausing, staring at the floor] I don't know.
MOM: [exasperated] What do you mean, "I don't know?"
JUNIOR: I don't know.

And so it goes. Depending on how long Mom's fuse is, Junior had better begin knowing something very soon! What is the problem here? Is it that Junior is simply refusing to talk? Probably not. He is simply being asked questions he cannot answer. He lacks the depth of understanding and self-reflection to be able to respond coherently to his mother's questions. He needs to have the issues focused in a different way.

The "Why did you . . ." line of questioning never works with children (and rarely with adults). Here are some more productive questions:

1. "What were you feeling when you hit your sister?"
2. "What did your sister do to make you mad?"
3. "Help me understand how hitting her seemed to make things better."
4. "What was the problem with what she was doing to you?" (You need not deny the fact your child has been sinned against. Perhaps he was sinned against. Let him tell you about it.)
5. "In what other ways could you have responded?"
6. "How do you think your response reflected trust or lack of trust in God's ability to care for and protect you?"

Each answer to these questions can open other avenues of pursuit in understanding what was behind Junior's behavior.

There are many different questions that address his sin and help him understand the Godward spiritual struggles of his heart and his need of Christ's grace and redemption. My point is this: You must begin by seeking to understand the nature of the internal conflict that was expressed in hitting his sister.

As he answers the above questions, your role is to help him understand himself and speak with clarity and honesty about his internal struggles with sin.

There are four issues you must walk him through: 1) the nature of temptation, 2) the possible responses to this temptation, 3) the motives for those responses, and 4) the sinful response he chose.

In this process you stand both above him and beside him. You are above him because God has called you to a role of discipline and correction. You are beside him because you, too, are a sinner who struggles with anger toward others.

Parents tend to do one or the other. Some stand in such solidarity with the child in his failure (asking, "How can I correct him when I do the same things?") that they fail to correct. Others stand so much above that they are hypocritically distanced from their children. You must remember that you engage your children in this manner as God's agent. You, therefore, have the right and obligation to censure evil. You do so as a sinner who is beside them and able to understand the way sin works in the human heart.

Having seen the importance of communication as one of the primary biblical methods of childrearing, we will turn in the next chapter to a description of various types of communication described in Scripture.

Application Questions for Chapter 8

1. Are you able to help your children express themselves?

2. What should be your first communication objective in responding to a problem with your children?

3. What are five or six good questions for drawing out what your child is thinking or feeling?

4. What changes would you have to make in your conversational style if you were going to have a conversation like the second example about the new sneakers?

5. Express in your own words what this statement means: "In the process of helping your child understand his sin, you stand both above him and beside him."

6. Do you understand the distinction drawn in this chapter between the "what" of behavior and the "why" of behavior?

Chapter

9

EMBRACING BIBLICAL METHODS: TYPES OF COMMUNICATION

*W*E OFTEN REDUCE parenting to these three elements: rules, correction, punishment. It could be pictured like this:

```
RULES
CORRECTION
DISCIPLINE
```

Figure 4 Parenting

This is how it works. You give your children the rules. The correction phase comes into play when they break the rules. In the punishment phase you announce the consequence they will receive for breaking the rules. Every family needs its rules, correction, and punishment, but for many this is the extent of communication.

This chapter discusses a rich dimension of communication that must lie beneath and support all you say in providing rules, calling your children to account and meting out appropriate discipline. The chart should look like this:

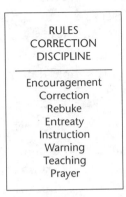

RULES
CORRECTION
DISCIPLINE

Encouragement
Correction
Rebuke
Entreaty
Instruction
Warning
Teaching
Prayer

Figure 5 Communication

On many occasions I have asked groups of parents what portion of their parenting communication was done through rules, correction, and punishment rather than these richer forms of communication. Most parents will quickly acknowledge that 80 to 90 percent of their communication is rules, correction, and punishment.

Types of Communication

Communication must be multifaceted and richly textured. It must include encouragement, correction, rebuke, entreaty, instruction, warning, teaching, and prayer. All of these must be part of your interaction with your children.

Paul instructs you in 1 Thessalonians 5 to modify your speech to suit the need of the moment: "Warn those who are idle, encourage the timid, help the weak, be patient with everyone" (1 Thessalonians 5:14). Paul's point is that differing conditions in the hearer require differing forms of speaking. You do great harm when you fail to discern what type of communication is appropriate to the moment.

I recall making the mistake of sharply rebuking one of my sons for looking sloppy. He was 7 or 8. It seemed to me that he looked as though he was always disheveled. I was not wrong for talking with him about his appearance, but I was wrong in rebuking him when he actually needed instruction. He was not rebelling. He had done nothing to deserve censure. He simply needed patient instruction. Days later, realizing I had wounded him, I had to seek his forgiveness for my undeserved rebuke.

Let's think through some simple definitions of various types of communication.

Encouragement

Children need communication designed to inspire and fill with hope and courage. I spoke one day with a youngster who had just exploded in anger at classmates. Calmed down, he was able to speak rationally. "It's no use," he said. "I just shouldn't play. Every time I do, someone makes me mad and this happens." This was obviously not a time for rebuke. This lad knew he was wrong. He had a sense of his inability to change fundamental features of his personality. What he needed was encouragement that Christ came because we are sinful people who cannot change ourselves. Rebuke, or even instruction, would have been inappropriate at the moment.

Your children know the pain of failure. They, like you, find things looking hopeless at times.

You can help them assess the reasons for disappointment. You need to help them understand the promises of God. You can encourage them to find courage, hope and inspiration from God, who draws near to the brokenhearted and contrite.

Correction

Sometimes a child needs to be brought into conformity with a standard. Correction remedies something wrong. Correction gives your children insight into what is wrong and what may be done to correct the problem. Correction helps your children to understand God's standard and teaches them to assess their behavior against that standard. 2 Timothy 3:16–17 reminds us that correction is one of the functions of the Word of God.

My wife, Margy, was having a conversation with our daughter one night. It was an occasion when the issue that prompted the talk became secondary because of what was happening during the conversation. Our daughter was playing the correction game like a pro. She was making all the right nods and comments. Her mother sensed, however, that Heather's heart was not joined to her head. Margy tested her suspicion by asking some probing questions. She quickly realized Heather's need for correction. She addressed Heather's response in terms of Proverbs 9 and the contrast between the way a mocker and a wise person receives correction. She administered correction, helping Heather to understand God's standard and assess her response to correction in terms of that standard. Heather's resistance quickly melted behind a torrent of tears. The conversation continued profitably.

Rebuke

A rebuke censures behavior. Sometimes a child must experience your sense of alarm, shock, and dismay at what he has done or said. For example, we have always taught our children that there are some necessary limits on free speech. We should never tell people we hate them, or wish death or injury upon them. Such statements would draw a stern rebuke. We would say with evident alarm and indignation, "It is wrong for you to speak those words. I never want to hear you speak in such a way again." (This would be followed, of course, by other forms of communication, such as instruction, encouragement, and prayer.)

Entreaty

This is communication that is earnest and intense. It involves pleading, soliciting, urging, and even begging. It is not, however, the begging of a beggar. It is rather the earnest pleading of a father or mother who, understanding his child, the ways of God, and the extremity of the moment, is willing to bare his soul in earnest pleading for his child to act in wisdom and faith. It is a special kind of communication that is reserved for use in cases of great import.

We get insight into entreaty in the Proverbs 23 passage quoted above. One cannot help hearing the earnest entreaty behind the words of Proverbs 23:26, "My son, give me your heart. . . ."

I have used this kind of communication in talking to my boys about the importance of avoiding sexual sins such as pornography. On scores of occasions I have entreated them about the danger of opening themselves to impurity. I have spoken about how sexual sin denigrates the image of God and fails to preserve his name as holy and glorious. I have warned that a life of sexual maladjustment is a high price to pay for fleeting moments of titillation. I have mixed my entreaty with encouragement that the joys of biblical sex within marriage are beautiful beyond description. (You will find a primer for this speech in Proverbs 5–7.) Obviously, I have not had conversations like this every day, but periodic entreaty about such important issues bears good fruit.

Instruction

Instruction is the process of providing a lesson, a precept, or information that will help your children to understand their world. As a parent, you are dealing with young people who have large gaps in their understanding of life. They need information about themselves and others. They need to understand the world of spiritual reality and the principles of the Kingdom of God.

Your children need a framework in which they can understand life. King Solomon's Proverbs are a rich source of information about life. The child who begins to understand the Proverbs' characterization of the fool, the sluggard, the wise man, the mocker, and so forth will develop discernment about life.

I was amazed to see my children interact with their high school experience with a depth of insight and perception I never knew while in high school. They have been able to evaluate their responses in ways I could not until my mid-20s. The reason? Instruction in the ways of God has given them biblical wisdom. This is what Psalm 119 is talking about:

Your commands make me wiser than my enemies,
    for they are ever with me.
I have more insight than all my teachers,
    for I meditate on your statutes.
I have more understanding than the elders,
    for I obey your precepts (119:98–100).

I gain understanding from your precepts;
    therefore I hate every wrong path (119:104).

Warning

Your children's lives are fraught with danger. Warnings put us on guard regarding a probable danger. A warning is merciful speech, for it is the equivalent of posting a sign informing motorists about a bridge that is out. A warning faithfully alerts us to danger while there is still time to escape unharmed. An alert parent can enable his child both to escape danger and learn in the process. Warning preserves.

The following proverbs contain warnings for the wise and discerning:

12:24   *". . . laziness ends in slave labor."*
13:18   *"He who ignores discipline comes to poverty and shame."*
14:23   *". . . mere talk leads only to poverty."*
15:1   *". . . a harsh word stirs up anger."*
16:18   *"Pride goes before destruction. . . ."*
17:19   *". . . he who builds a high gate invites destruction."*
19:15   *". . . the shiftless man goes hungry."*

This is only a suggestive list of warnings from Proverbs.

One of the most powerful ways we can warn our children is to fill their heads with the cautions of the Bible.

How do the warnings work? A warning is simply a statement that A leads to B. For example, laziness leads to slavery. The person who is lazy will end up in some form of servitude. The warning is an application of the sowing and reaping principle that we find operative throughout Scripture. Warning your children is not a matter of yelling some pithy saying at them when they are leaving the house to go somewhere. It is acquainting them with the sowing-and-reaping principle found throughout Scripture. It is spending time helping them understand the many A-leads-to-B statements of Scripture.

Eventually, they will begin to understand and embrace these things. Once your children begin to internalize such truths, their attitudes and behaviors are powerfully influenced.

Our daughter's early school years were spent homeschooling and in a small Christian school, but she later attended a public high school. When we dropped her off at the school for the first day we had a lump in our throats. As we watched her pass through the doors into this large school, we knew that she would feel alone.

As the days went by, it was the warnings and encouragements of the Proverbs that enabled her to form good friendships. The Proverbs warn (14:7) about fools and instruct us to stay away from them. They also identify a fool. A fool shows his annoyance at once (12:16). Whoever spreads slander is a fool (10:18). These and many other warnings gave her the basis for wise discrimination in forming friendships. Though she had never been in a large school, the Scriptures prepared her for making wise choices.

How does that process work out in practice? There were conversations like this:

TINA: Hi, you're the new girl aren't you? What's your name?

HEATHER: Heather.

TINA: Hi, I'm Tina. Come and eat lunch with me. I'll tell you all about this school.

HEATHER: Oh, okay.

TINA: Do you see this girl coming with the tray? She is Christine. She's real popular. She thinks she's great because she has nice clothes and her boyfriend is a football player. I can't stand her . . . Oh, hi, Christine. This is my friend Heather.

What is Heather learning? Tina is a slanderer. While she has broken the ice with Heather, she is not someone whom Heather can trust. Insight from Proverbs has prepared Heather to make a discerning evaluation of this girl. The warnings she has received and internalized as part of her value system have given her discernment.

Teaching

Teaching is the process of imparting knowledge. Teaching is causing someone to know something. Sometimes, teaching takes place before it is needed. It is often most powerfully done after a failure or problem. As a godly parent, you have much to impart. Drawing upon knowledge of Scripture, you may teach your child to understand himself, others, life, God's revelation, and the world. You must actively impart knowledge to your children.

Prayer

While prayer is not communication with the child but with God, it is nevertheless an essential element of communication between the parent and the child. Our most penetrating insights into our children will often come as they pray. Understanding what they pray and how they pray is often a window into their souls. In the same manner, the parent's prayer provides instruction and insight for the child. I am not suggesting that you pray for the child's consumption, but that you recognize that hearing your prayer will communicate your faith in God to your child.

Summary

This is the point: Your communication with your children will take many forms. The subtle and rich nuances of each of the forms of communication outlined above must be reflected in your communication with your children.

Each of the elements of this suggestive (by no means exhaustive) list will be interwoven with the others to provide a rich tapestry of communication.

For example, you may entreat in a way that warns or in a way that encourages. Or you may instruct in a manner that rebukes or in a manner that corrects. The elements of communication may be woven together in many ways.

Application Questions for Chapter 9

1. What proportion of your communication is restricted to the top block of figure 5?

2. When you find problems at home, do you expect to solve them with a new set of rules and punishments, or with richer forms of communication?

3. Outline how you would talk to your teen who seemed to have stolen some money from you but would not admit it.

4. What are the "quality of relationship" issues that must be in place if you are going to be able to entreat your child in winsome ways?

5. How would you encourage your child who had failed miserably but seemed genuinely to desire God's help?

6. Of the nine types of communication mentioned in this chapter, at which ones are you most proficient? At which ones are you least proficient?

7. Ultimately, communication is a reflection of the heart. "For out of the overflow of his heart his mouth speaks" (Luke 6:45). What are the "overflow of the heart" issues that impact your ability to communicate effectively?

EMBRACING BIBLICAL METHODS: A LIFE OF COMMUNICATION

IN 1978, OUR FAMILY built a house. As we worked, we talked about things we would do when we finished building the house. In the intervening years, we have put on an addition, remodeled the bathroom and kitchen, and are preparing to dig for another addition. We no longer talk about finishing the house. We realize that we will always be retrofitting our home. There will always be some improvement to be made.

Building our house has become more than an event in our life as a family—it has become a lifestyle! Communication is like that.

A Life of Communication

Communication not only disciplines, it also disciples. It shepherds your children in the ways of God. Like the teaching of Deuteronomy 6, this full-orbed communication occurs while lying down, waking, rising, walking, and sitting. Parents are often too busy to talk unless something is wrong. A regular habit of talking together prepares the way for talking in strained situations. You will never have the hearts of your children if you talk with them only when something has gone wrong.

Shepherding the Heart

I have used the phrase "shepherding the heart" to embody the process of guiding our children. It means helping them understand themselves, God's works, the ways of God, how sin works in the human heart, and how the gospel comes to them at the most profound levels of human need. Shepherding the hearts of children also involves helping them understand their motivations, goals, wants, wishes, and desires. It exposes the true nature of reality and encourages faith in the Lord Jesus Christ. You undertake the shepherding process through the kind of rich, multifaceted communication that I have sketched here. Later chapters will add color and texture to what has already been sketched briefly in earlier chapters.

Counting the Cost

Honest, thorough, truly biblical communication is expensive. Insightful and penetrating conversations take time. Children require both time and flexibility. Children do not pour their hearts out or open themselves up on a demand schedule. A wise parent talks when the kids are in the mood. Every so often they will ask a question, make a comment, reveal some little aspect of their heart. In those times, when their conscience is stirred, you need to talk. This may require dropping everything else to seize a critical moment.

You must become a good listener. You will miss precious opportunities when you only half-listen to your children. The best way you can train your children to be active listeners is by actively listening to them.

Some people think listening is what you do between opportunities to say something. During listening times they don't listen at all.

They are deciding what to say. Don't be such a parent. The Proverbs remind you that the fool does not delight in understanding, but in airing his own opinion (Proverbs 18:2).

It is certainly hard to know when to be quiet and listen, but no one said parenting would be easy. Work at it. Stop sometimes and think about what you have heard. Think, too, about what you have not heard. Stopping and listening provides time to pray silently, to refocus and be creative in your conversation.

Good communication is expensive in other areas. The stamina and spiritual energy that searching conversation requires often seems overwhelming. Parents sometimes miss valuable opportunities because they feel too tired to follow through.

We began to experience this physical dimension very clearly when our children became teens. We had been in the habit of putting little ones to bed in the early evening. This gave us time for conversation. But with teens came later nights. I am not sure why, but many times the greatest opportunities for communication came late at night. The wise parent talks when the kids are ready to talk!

Proper communication requires mental stamina. You must keep your thoughts focused. You must avoid the temptations to chase unimportant matters. Questions that have not been answered must be posed in new and fresh ways.

You must bring integrity to your interaction with your children. You model the dynamics of the Christian life for your children. You must let them see sonship with the Father in you. You should show them repentance. Acknowledge your joys and fears and how you find comfort in God. Live a shared life of repentance and thankfulness. Acknowledge your own sin and weakness. Admit when you are wrong. Be prepared to seek forgiveness for sinning against your children. The right to make searching and honest appraisal of your children lies in willingness to do the same for yourself.

Recently, a father of three children recounted a situation in which he had sinned against his son. He had spoken cruelly and struck his son in an abusive way. He seemed very broken over his sin. When I asked what his son said when he sought forgiveness, he acknowledged that he had not sought his son's forgiveness. This dad will never have open communication with his son until he is willing to humble himself and acknowledge his own sin. If he won't do that, the attempt to talk about the things of God is a sham.

Counting the Blessings of Paying the Cost

In business, it is customary to run a cost vs. benefit analysis. The purpose of an analysis is to ascertain if the benefits (in our case—blessings) are great enough to justify the cost. Let us now consider some of the real blessings for which we incur these costs.

Parent-Child Relationship

Full-orbed, rich, multifaceted communication is the cement that holds a parent and a child together. Communication will provide the context for a growing unity with your children. Children know when they have a relationship with people who are wise and discerning, who know and understand them, who love and are committed to them. They will know if you know the ways of God, understand life and people in the world, and are prepared to carry on a relationship of integrity and security. There will be times of disagreement or conflict, but disagreement can be resolved in a relationship of open communication.

Pressures of the teen years pull children away from home. This is the time when they develop camaraderie with those who "understand them." They are looking for relationships in which someone knows, understands, and loves them. Your children should not have to leave home for that. You can provide family relationships in which your children are understood and embraced.

The attraction the "wrong crowd" holds is not a license for being bad. The attraction of the "wrong crowd" is camaraderie. Children long to be known, understood, discipled and loved.

I think of biblical childrearing in the following terms:

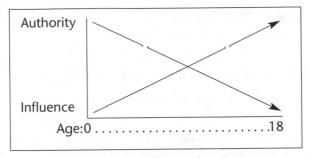

Figure 6 Authority/Influence Continuum

I am using the term authority a little differently here. Authority here denotes what may be accomplished with your child because you are stronger, faster, larger, and so forth. What parents with newborn children may accomplish simply because they are in charge—because they are the authorities—is at an all-time high. They call all the shots. Baby may cry in protest, but Mom and Dad have the initiative. Even the young toddler is somewhat intimidated by size. Parents may buttress commands—"I told you to sit down!"—by physically placing him in the chair. The parents' word is law because they have the physical capacity to enforce it.

As a child grows, the ability to control him that way diminishes. The more Junior grows and develops physically and mentally, what you may accomplish through raw authority diminishes.

Imagine the following scenario. I go into the room of my 16-year-old son to wake him for school and he says, "I ain't goin'." What am I to do? While I have a small weight advantage, he is stronger than I am. Even if I could wrestle him out of bed, dress him in spite of his protests, and get him on the school bus (all highly doubtful), what have I accomplished? He can get off the bus at the next stop. If he stays on, I have no guarantee he will remain in school.

I am thankful that my son has never done this, but my point is this: I can no longer secure obedience through superior size. My ability to require obedience because I am stronger has been eroding since the day he was born.

While I am limited in what I can accomplish through the raw use of authority, thankfully, my son is willingly under my influence.

In this chart, influence represents the willingness of a child to place himself under authority because of trust. This trust has several elements. Children trust you when they know you love them and are committed to their good, when they know you understand them, when they know you understand their strengths and weaknesses, when they know that you have invested yourself in encouragement, correction, rebuke, entreaty, instruction, warning, understanding, teaching, and prayer. When a child knows that all his life you have sought to see the world through his eyes, he will trust you. When he knows that you have not tried to make him like you or like anybody else, but only sought to help him realize his full potential as a creature God made to know him and live in the relationship of fellowship with him, he will trust you.

The result is obvious: Your words will have weight. What child would walk away from such a relationship? You have influence with him. Each day you live with your children, your influence grows. As children learn about life, they learn to trust their father and mother more. Mother gives warnings about relationships and insightful suggestions about how to be God's person in a world that requires conformity. They try it and it works because it is based on biblical wisdom. Each day children live, they grow in their understanding of the nurturing care and love of their parents.

Imagine that I was the most trusted adviser of the president of the United States. Imagine that he never made a decision and never did anything other than what I suggested. How much authority would I have in the government? None. I have no elected office. No one is required to listen to me. How much influence would I have? A great deal, perhaps more than anyone else.

As you engage your children in the rich, full communication described above, you not only nurture them, but develop a relationship of unity and trust.

Preparation for Relationships

Your children will need finely honed communication skills for every relationship they will ever have. As workers, whether in the position of an employer or employee, they must understand others and express their thoughts to others. As husbands or wives, they need the same abilities. As consumers, citizens, members of the body of Christ, parents—in every stage and station of life—they must learn to speak with precision and accuracy. They must gain facility in drawing others out.

Communication is the art of expressing in godly ways what is in my heart and of hearing completely and understanding what another thinks and feels.

Home is the place for developing these skills. What a great advantage for the child who has learned to articulate his thoughts and to understand others.

Every time you tenderly draw the deepest wishes, hopes, thoughts, ideas, and desires out of your children, you become an example of how to serve in this important area of relationship.

Full-Orbed Understanding of Life

Sensitive communication with your children enables them to understand the complexity of life. They learn that life is concerned with both the world of feelings and the world of ideas. It means understanding yourself and others. It means having long-term vision as well as short-term goals. It's being concerned with not only the "what" or "what happened," but also about the "why."

It means seeing character development as more important than short-term gratification. Only biblical communication will expose these important life issues. The more you talk with your children, helping them to understand themselves, their temptations, fears and doubts, the more you prepare them to understand life in the world.

Redemption Integrated with Life

All this communication gives children a biblical understanding of mankind. It gives them a better understanding of themselves. It helps them understand God's standard. They learn that God is ultimate. This provides a biblical grid for understanding life. They learn that humanity's problem is sin. We all sin and are sinned against. We are both perpetrators and victims. For this reason, all of life must be viewed in terms of God's redemptive restoration of man.

They see the centrality of the gospel of grace. Jesus Christ came to this earth and lived the life that all men and women should live. He fully obeyed the law of God, and through faith his obedience can be imputed to them. They learn that in Jesus one can find forgiveness, renewal, and empowerment. The more profoundly they know themselves and their neediness, the more deeply they will understand their need of the internal change and power that grace brings.

They see how knowing and loving God—finding grace, power, and fullness in him—answers their deepest needs. All of life is lived through the power and grace of the gospel. Christ is relevant everywhere for everything.

In this way, your kids are provided with a grid through which to filter the events of life when you're not there to provide direction and correction They are trained to be independent, trained to stand on their own without parental support. What better training is there than to equip your child to understand life through a biblical, redemptive grid?

Children can go off to college and develop nurturing relationships both with fellow students and with the Christian community. We should not be surprised; they are simply finding new relationships like the ones they have enjoyed at home.

Is It Worth the Cost?

The benefits are great, and doubtless other benefits could be deduced. Every parent wants the things outlined above for his child. But what about the costs?

To be sure, these things do not come cheap. The cost is great. It requires being available and fully engaged in parenting.

There is a simple way to look at the cost of deep, full-orbed communication. You must regard parenting as one of your most important tasks while you have children at home. This is your calling. You must raise your children in the fear and admonition of the Lord. You cannot do so without investing yourself in a life of sensitive communication in which you help them understand life and God's world. There is nothing more important. You have only a brief season of life to invest yourself in this task. You have only one opportunity to do it. You cannot go back and do it over.

You live in a culture in which there are opportunities for you to do things unheard of in history. You are presented daily with scores of options for investing your life's energies and creatvity. There is more than you could ever do. You must, therefore, prioritize.

Parenting is your primary calling. Parenting will mean that you can't do all the things that you could otherwise do. It will affect your golf handicap. It may mean your home does not look like a picture from *Better Homes and Gardens*. It will impact your career and ascent on the corporate ladder. It will alter the kind of friendships you will be available to pursue. It will influence the kind of ministry you are able to pursue. It will modify the amount of time you have for bowling, hunting, television, or how many books you read. It will mean that you can't develop every interest that comes along. The costs are high.

How can you measure the cost against the benefits? I have spent time with broken parents. I have seen the drawn faces of parents who have known the heartbreak of seeing their children fleeing a home in which they had not been understood or engaged by their parents. I have also known the joy of hearing children who have been biblically engaged by their parents say, "Dad, I am amazed at how thoroughly I have been prepared for life. I will always be grateful for what you and Mom have given me." What price tag can a parent place on that?

God calls you to invest yourself in this way with your children. This kind of communication is not just beneficial, it is mandated! It is the path of blessing because it is the path of obedience. Is this kind of communication expensive? Yes! But the benefits far exceed the cost.

In the beginning of chapter 7, I laid out two methods for childrearing—communication and the rod. In the next chapter we will look at the place of the rod in biblical parenting.

———— *Application Questions for Chapter 10* ————

1. If you were to have the kind of communication with your children outlined here, what would the costs be for you? Are you willing to pay that price?

2. How are you at hearing what your child is saying?

3. Is confession of your sins, where appropriate, a regular part of your communication with your children?

4. What are the sanctification issues that you would need to address in order to lead your children in the ways set forth in this chapter?

5. How can you help your children have a vision for the kind of communication outlined in this chapter?

11

EMBRACING BIBLICAL METHODS: THE ROD

*T*HE SINCERE ENTREATY accenting every syllable caught my ear. "Dear, you know what Mommy said and you did not obey Mommy. And now I'll have to spank you. You know, Dear, that I am not mad at you, but you must learn to obey."

The baby was mute in the face of correction, but then she was only a doll. And the mommy? She was 4-year-old Lauren. The speaker behind the speaker was obviously her mother.

Lauren learned how to discipline dollies from her mother disciplining her. Lauren imitates Mommy. Her mother understands that Lauren possesses abilities not found in dollies. She knows that Lauren's behavior has a moral dimension. Lauren is not ethically neutral. Lauren's misbehavior brings her into conflict with God's law. Her heart trades in issues of good and evil. Mother understands, too, that the issues of correction transcend the present. All earthly punishment presupposes the great day when destinies are eternally fixed. Mother wants her to be ready for that.

As I listened to this little 4-year-old, the clear structure and gracious manner of this make-believe discipline session impressed me. The lines were well-rehearsed. Lauren had heard them many times. There was no anger, only firmness in her voice as she prepared her baby for what was to come. The objective was also clear—"You must learn to obey." There was nothing in the manner of this young imitator of "Mommy" that looked or sounded like child abuse. Yet our culture regards all corporal punishment as cruel and abusive. For some parents it may be a reaction to ways they were abused. For most of us it is a matter of style.

I can understand the resistance of many parents to corporal discipline. Perhaps they themselves were abused. Maybe they experienced discipline that was an expression of unbridled anger. They were struck on-the-fly by parents who were venting anger and frustration. As children, they may have expereinced fear, hurt, and cruel abuse. Perhaps they thought, "When I am a parent, I will never do that to my kids."

To all such parents, I say, "I heartily agree with your determination not to do to your children what your parents did to you. If you experienced such abusive treatment, it was wrong and certainly should never be done to your kids."

But I fear the majority reaction against spanking is a matter of fashion or style. The world of ideas is continually in flux. Ideas have their periods of popularity and unpopularity. Like color combinations that go in and out of vogue in the world of fashion and decorating, ideas go in and out of style.

The rod, as a form of discipline, is an idea that is unfashionable at present. If I had written this book in the 1950s, the section on communication would have gotten little attention from the average man. No one talked with children then. They were trotted, John Wayne-style, to the woodshed. Dad was the strong, silent type who did not talk much, but who used his brawn to keep his boy in line.

We live in an era when concepts of human rights and dignity have been used to argue that spanking children is barbaric. We have become sensitive to the potential for child abuse. We don't want parents to feel it is their right to beat their children whenever they wish. Today, communication based on integrity and mutual respect is a more popular idea. Therefore, it is easier to write about that.

The Rationale Behind the Rod

Many questions about spanking children flood our minds. What is it designed to accomplish? Is it really necessary? Isn't there a better way? What is the idea behind it? Will it make your children resent you?

Nick, a friend from church, and his girlfriend, Angela, were visiting for a Sunday afternoon. During our meal, one of our sons was disobedient. I took him to a private room upstairs to discipline him.

"What's he going to do with him?" Angela inquired.

"Probably spank him," my wife responded matter-of-factly.

At that moment my son's cry could be heard upstairs. Angela went running from the house in a state of great agitation.

What was her problem? She did not understand spanking biblically, so she felt offended and concerned about what, to her, appeared to be parental cruelty. Her attitude was not unusual.

The Nature of the Problem

What is the nature of the child's most basic need? If children are born ethically and morally neutral, then they do not need correction; they need direction. They do not need discipline; they need instruction.

Certainly, children need instruction and direction. But is their most basic problem a lack of information? Are all the problems gone once they are able to learn a few things? Of course not!

Children are not born morally and ethically neutral. The Bible teaches that the heart is "deceitful and desperately wicked" (Jeremiah 17:9, KJV). The child's problem is not an information deficit. His problem is that he is a sinner. There are things within the heart of

the sweetest little baby that, allowed to blossom and grow to fruition, will bring about eventual destruction.

The rod functions in this context. It is addressed to needs within
the child. These needs cannot be met by mere talk. Proverbs 22:15
says, "Folly is bound up in the heart of a child, but the rod of
discipline will drive it far from him." God says there is something
wrong in the child's heart. Folly or foolishness is bound up in his
heart. This folly must be removed, for it places the child at risk.

When we speak of folly we are not speaking of childishness.
Children do childish things. They spill the milk at the breakfast
table. (If you have young children you must plan on mopping up
gallons of milk.) They try to give their teddy bear a drink of their
orange juice. We don't discipline for childishness even when it is
terribly inconvenient.

Throughout the Proverbs, folly/foolishness is used to describe the
person who has no fear of God. The fool is the one who will not
hear reproof. The fool is the one who will not submit to authority.
The fool is the one who mocks at the ways of God. The fool lacks
wisdom (fear of the Lord). "The fool has said in his heart, 'there
is no God'" (Psalm 14:1). The fool says, "I refuse to acknowledge
God; there is no God to be concerned with; my only concern is
myself and my agenda."

The fool's life is run by his desires and fears. This is what you
hear from your young children. The most common phrases in the
vocabulary of a 3-year-old are, "I want . . ." or "I don't want. . . ."
The fool lives out of the immediacy of his lusts, cravings, expectations, hopes, and fears.

It is a question of authority. Will the child live under the authority of God and therefore the authority of his parents, or under his
own authority—driven by his wants and passions?

This is the natural state of your children. It may be subtly hidden beneath a tuft of rumpled hair. It may be imperceptible in the
smile of a baby. In their natural state, however, your children have
hearts of folly. Therefore, they resist correction. They protest against
your attempts to rule them. Watch a baby struggle against a diaper

change or wearing a hat in the winter. Even this baby who cannot articulate or even conceptualize what he is doing shows a determination not to be ruled from without. This foolishness is bound up within his heart. Allowed to take root and grow for fourteen or fifteen years, it will produce a rebellious teenager who will not allow anyone to rule him.

God has ordained the rod of discipline for this condition. The spanking process (undertaken in a biblical manner set forth in chapter 15) drives foolishness from the heart of a child. Confrontation, with the immediate and undeniably tactile sensation of a spanking, renders an implacable child sweet. I have seen this principle hold true countless times. The young child who is refusing to be under authority is in a place of grave danger.

The rod is given for this extremity. "Punish him [a child] with the rod and save his soul from death" (Proverbs 23:14). Your children's souls are in danger of death—spiritual death. Your task is to rescue your children from death. Faithful and timely use of the rod is the means of rescue.

This places the rod in its proper setting. Use of the rod is not a matter of an angry parent venting his wrath upon a small, helpless child. The use of the rod signifies a faithful parent recognizing his child's dangerous state and employing a God-given remedy. The issue is not a parental insistence on being obeyed. The issue is the child's need to be rescued from death—the death that results from rebellion left unchallenged in the heart.

The Function of the Rod

What does the rod of correction do for the child? How does it work? In Proverbs 29:15 God says, "The rod of correction imparts wisdom. . . ." Elsewhere, the Proverbs connect wisdom with the fear of the Lord. Fearing God and acquiring wisdom come through the instrumentality of the rod.

The connection of the rod with wisdom is of profound importance. The child who is not submitting to parental authority is acting foolishly. He is rejecting the jurisdiction of God. He is living his life for the immediate gratification of his wants and desires. Ultimately, to refuse God's rule means to choose his own rule that leads to death. It is the height of foolishness.

The rod of correction brings wisdom to the child. It provides an immediate tactile demonstration of the foolishness of rebellion. Properly administered discipline humbles the heart of a child, making him subject to parental instruction. An atmosphere is created in which instruction can be given. The spanking renders the child compliant and ready to receive life-giving words.

Hebrews 12:11 puts it this way: "No discipline seems pleasant at the time, but painful. Later on, however, it produces a harvest of righteousness and peace for those who have been trained by it."

The rod of discipline, while it brings pain, also brings a harvest of righteousness and peace. The child whose parents use the rod in a timely, appropriate fashion learns to submit to authority.

Don't all kids learn to obey eventually? Not according to the Proverbs. "The rod of correction imparts wisdom, but a child left to himself disgraces his mother. Discipline your son, and he will give you peace; he will bring delight to your soul" (Proverbs 29:15, 17).

God has commanded the use of the rod in discipline and correction of children. It is not the only thing you do, but it must be used. He has told you that there are needs within your children that require the use of the rod. If you are going to rescue your children from death, if you are going to root out the folly that is bound up in their hearts, if you are going to impart wisdom, you must use the rod.

What is the Rod?

The rod is a parent, in faith toward God and faithfulness toward his or her children, undertaking the responsibility of careful, timely, measured, and controlled use of physical punishment to underscore the importance of obeying God, thus rescuing the child from continuing in his foolishness until death.

A Parental Exercise

Let's look at the elements of this definition. By definition, the rod is a parental exercise. All the passages that urge the use of the rod place it in the protected context of the parent-child relationship. The command is "discipline your son." The Bible does not grant permission to all adults to engage in corporal punishment of all children. It is an element in a broader range of parenting activities. It does not stand alone.

This is one of the problems with spanking children at school. When a teacher undertakes the spanking, the spanking process is removed from its context in the parent-child relationship. The same mother and father who comfort the child when he is sick, who take him to amusement parks, who remember his birthday, give the spanking. A spanking is very different when administered by a non-parent.

An Act of Faith

The use of the rod is an act of faith. God has mandated its use. The parent obeys, not because he perfectly understands how it works, but because God has commanded it. The use of the rod is a profound expression of confidence in God's wisdom and the excellence of his counsel.

An Act of Faithfulness

The rod is an act of faithfulness toward a child. Recognizing that in discipline there is hope, and refusing to be a willing party to his child's death, the parent undertakes the task. It is an expression of love and commitment.

On many occasions, my children have seen tears in my eyes when it was time to spank them. I did not want to do it. My love for my children drove me to the task. I would have never spanked them had I not been persuaded by the Word of God that God called me to this task. It is not my personality. Margy and I were exposed to some teaching from the book of Proverbs that convinced us that spanking had a valid place in parenting. We became persuaded that failure to spank would be unfaithfulness to their souls.

A Responsibility

The rod is a responsibility. It is not the parent determining to punish. It is the parent determining to obey. It is the parent, as God's representative, undertaking on God's behalf what God has called him to do. He is not on his own errand, but fulfilling God's.

A Physical Punishment

The rod is the careful, timely, measured and controlled use of physical punishment. The rod is never a venting of parental anger. It is not what the parent does when he is frustrated. It is not a response to feeling that his child has made things hard for him. It is always measured and controlled. The parent knows the proper measure of severity for this particular child at this particular time. The child knows how many swats are to come.

A Rescue Mission

The rod is a rescue mission. The child who needs a spanking has become distanced from his parents through disobedience. The spanking is designed to rescue the child from continuing in his foolishness. If he continues, his doom is certain. Thus, the parent, driven by love for the child, must use the rod.

The rod underscores the importance of obeying God. Remember, the issue is never, "You have failed to obey ME." The only reason for a child to obey Mom and Dad is that God commands it. Failure to obey Mom or Dad is, therefore, failure to obey God. This is the issue. The child has failed to obey God. The child has failed to do what God has mandated. To persist places the child at great risk. It is not a kindness for the parent to ignore the rebellion against God's authority that will ultimately bring God's even greater chastisement.

Distortions of the Rod

Since the rod is an idea that has fallen on hard times in our culture, we need to clear our minds of some distorted concepts of the rod. I do not want you to think I am advocating one of the popular misconceptions of the rod. Here are some things the rod is not:

Not the Right to Unbridled Temper

The biblical concept of the rod is not the right to unbridled temper. As we will discuss more fully in the second section of this book, the rod must be used in the most carefully guarded, tightly structured manner to avoid the possibility of abuse. Nowhere does God give parents the right to throw temper fits at their children. Such rage is ungodly and wicked. The Bible censures it. James 1:20 says: "Man's anger does not bring about the righteous life that God desires."

Not the Right to Hit Our Children Whenever We Wish

The biblical concept of the rod is not the right to hit our children whenever we wish. The rod is used in the context of correction and discipline. Again, it is not the right to use physical force whenever and however one wishes. God warns against the danger of embittering children in Ephesians 6. The parent who bullies his child physically will surely embitter him.

Not Venting of Frustration

The biblical concept of the rod is not a way for parents to vent their frustration with their children. I have never met a parent who has not had moments of frustration with his children. There are times when they exasperate you, leaving you hurt and angry. The rod is not a way for you to vent your pent-up rage and frustration.

Not Retribution

The biblical concept of the rod is not the parent exacting retribution for the child's wrong. It is not payment due. Many parents have a punitive mindset. They see discipline as the child paying for his sins. Rather than correction having the positive goal of restoration, it has the negative goal of payment. It is like the convict paying his debt to society by doing time in prison. This is not a biblical concept of discipline.

Not Associated with Vindictive Anger

Another distortion is the notion that the rod must be associated with vindictive anger. A friend of mine had to spank his son during a visit with his folks. He took his child into a private room, spoke with him and administered a spanking. Afterward, he reassured his son of his love for him. Smiling together, they emerged from the room. The spanking was over. The son was restored to his father. They were both happy and at peace. The grandmother, however, was upset. The spanking did not bother her. It was the fact my friend was not angry and distanced from him that troubled her. She said a spanking would do no good unless they were mad at each other afterward. She saw spankings as something that produced distance rather than closeness.

I know that there is such a thing as righteous indignation, although I think it is not well understood. People tend to think, "I am right and I am indignant, therefore this is righteous indignation." The difference between righteous and unrighteous indignation is illustrated by asking, "Whose honor is being preserved?" If I am angry because God has been dishonored and that vexes me, I am probably experiencing righteous anger. If my anger is the garden variety, "I can't believe you're doing this to me, who do you think you are, you little brat," it is probably unrighteous anger. That kind of anger will muddy the waters of discipline.

Common Objections to the Rod

I Love My Children Too Much to Spank Them

This objection is easy to understand. I know of nothing harder than spanking my children. It is difficult to hold your own child over your knee and be the cause of his discomfort. You feel that you love him too much to do so. But ask yourself this question: Who benefits if you do not spank your child? Surely not the child. The above passages make it clear that such failure places the child at risk. Who benefits? You do. You are delivered from the discomfort of spanking your child. You are delivered from the agony of causing discomfort for this one who is precious to you. You are delivered from the inconvenience and loss of time that biblical discipline requires. I believe this is why the Bible says in Proverbs 13:24: "He who spares the rod hates his son, but he who loves him is careful to discipline him." According to this passage, it is hatred, not love, that will keep me from spanking my child. Love will force me to do it.

I'm Afraid I Will Hurt Him

Often Christian parents respond negatively to the biblical concept of the "rod" because they have endured abusive corporal punishment in their childhood. The term rod brings to their minds angry parents flailing their children in an uncontrolled rage. Such behavior is not a biblical use of the rod. It is child abuse.

Some parents are apprehensive about hurting their children. They fear that some physical damage may result from corporal punishment. Proverbs 23:13–14 anticipates this objection. "Do not withhold discipline from a child; if you punish him with the rod, he will not die. Punish him with the rod and save his soul from death."

Biblically-balanced discipline never physically endangers a child.

I'm Afraid It Will Make Him Rebellious and Angry

As a parent, you want your children to love and appreciate you. You want them to think Mom and Dad are great. You want them to feel you are loving and kind. You may fear that spanking will make them think of you as cruel and harsh. You may fear that discipline will bring out the worst in them. Proverbs 29:17 states the opposite: "Discipline your son, and he will give you peace; he will bring delight to your soul."

Rather than discipline yielding angry, sullen children, it yields children who are at peace with you. It produces children in whom you delight.

This is true not only in the long term, but also in the short term. Administering a spanking in the manner laid out in chapter 15 yields a child who is engaged and happy—even immediately after a spanking.

I am Afraid of Teaching Them to Hit

Many parents worry that spanking will model hitting as a means of solving problems. The danger of children seeing hitting as an appropriate response to frustration will arise only if parents are spanking in anger. If the procedure outlined for spanking in chapter 15 is followed, the spanking will never be an expression of anger or frustration. Children will be able to recognize that what they do when they strike someone in anger is very different from the patient and gracious use of the rod outlined in this book.

It Doesn't Work

This objection requires further examination of a parent's specific practice. Years of pastoral experience have persuaded me that cases of the rod not working can be summarized as follows:

A) The primary reason spanking can be ineffective is spanking in anger. Children will not willingly submit themselves to the authority of an angry, out-of-control parent. There is an innate sense of justice in a child; they will inwardly resist submitting their hearts to a parent who bullies them. They may cower. They may even respond to the punishment out of fear, but they will not willingly place themselves under the authority of a parent who disciplines in unholy anger.

B) Inconsistent use of the rod. The child never knew what would elicit a spanking. Therefore, he was always testing the parent.

C) Failure to persist. Some folks never try anything long enough for it to work. They give the rod a couple of days. Their children are not transformed overnight. They give up in discouragement.

D) Failure to be effective. I have witnessed spankings administered through a double layer of diapers to a child who never stopped moving long enough to know he had been spanked. The spanking was ineffective because the parents never made the rod felt.

I'm Afraid of Being Arrested for Child Abuse

There is measure of validity to this concern, although it is not illegal to spank your children. What is illegal is child abuse, but a properly administered spanking is not abusive. Obviously, in a society which does not understand the Bible and equates spanking with abuse, one must be wise. Spanking should be done in the privacy of the home. It should not be a public matter. I might add here that public spanking may add the idea of "shaming" to a spanking that should be a private three-way event —God, parent, and child.

There may be circumstances outside the home in which you choose to overlook behavior that you would not overlook if you were at home. Parents have sometimes said to me, "If I make it a habit not to discipline when we are away from home, my children will know that and be impossible to handle." When dealing with young children, most of the time you will be at home and will have plenty of opportunities to deal with these issues. You can always leave wherever you are and go home if the issues are important enough to necessitate leaving.

The Fruit of the Rod

The rod teaches outcomes to behavior. Consistent use of the rod teaches your children to develop a harvest mentality; they learn that they will reap what they sow. Young children must learn to obey. When disobedience is met with uncomfortable consequences, they learn that God has built the principle of sowing and reaping into their world.

The rod shows God's authority over Mom and Dad. The parent who uses the rod as a matter of obedience is being an example of submission to authority. One of the reasons children have difficulty with authority is that they do not see it modeled in our culture.

The rod trains a child to be under authority. The fact that there are certain consequences to disobedience teaches the importance of obedience. The child learns while still young that God has placed everyone under authority and that authority structures are a blessing.

The rod demonstrates parental love and commitment. Hebrews 12 makes it clear that the rod is an expression of love. In verse 5, discipline is a sign of sonship. The parent who disciplines shows he loves his child. He is not an uninterested party. He is not ambivalent. He is engaged and involved. His commitment runs deep—deep enough to invest himself in careful discipline.

The rod yields a harvest of peace and righteousness. In Hebrews 12:11 we read, "No discipline seems pleasant at the time, but painful. Later on, however, it produces a harvest of righteousness and peace for those who have been trained by it." Timely, careful discipline, while unpleasant and painful at the time, yields happy, successful children.

The rod bears wonderful fruit. As a father of adult children, I am continually thankful for God's mercy to our family. Our first exposure to the ideas that are set out in this chapter came when we had only one child. He was an unruly 18-month-old who was on his way to the terrible two's! These principles gave us a way to deal with our son. They enabled us to give him the security of discipline. They enabled him to gain self-control. They helped him to respect and love his mom and dad.

The rod returns the child to the place of blessing. Left to himself, he would continue to live a lust-driven life. He would continue to seek comfort in being a slave to his desires and fears. The rod of correction returns him to the place of submission to parents in which God has promised blessing.

The rod promotes an atmosphere of closeness and openness between parent and child. The parent who is engaging his child and refusing to ignore things that challenge the integrity of their relationship will experience intimacy with his child. When a child is allowed to be sullen and disobedient, distance develops between the parent and child. The parent who refuses to allow estrangement will enjoy a close and open relationship.

The Best of Both

If you focus exclusively on either the rod or communication, you will be like a ship with all the cargo loaded on one side. You won't sail very well. Communication and the rod are not stand-alone methods. They are designed to work together.

This is the point of Hebrews 12:5–6: "You have forgotten that word of encouragement that addresses you as sons: 'My son, do not make light of the Lord's discipline, and do not lose heart when he rebukes you, because the Lord disciplines those he loves, and he punishes everyone he accepts as a son.' "

Your children need to be known and understood—thus rich communication is necessary. They also need authority. They need limits that are clear and correction that is predictable—thus the rod is necessary.

The use of the rod preserves biblically rooted, parental authority. The emphasis on rich communication prohibits cold, tyrannical discipline.

Obviously, the primacy of one or the other of these methods will depend on the ages of your children. We will focus on this in greater depth in the second part of this book.

Some parents have a greater facility for either communication or the rod. It is good to be sensitive to the nonbiblical distortions of each. The person who is comfortable with the rod can fall into the distortion of being authoritarian. A parent for whom communication is natural and easy may tend toward permissiveness. Authoritarian parents tend to lack kindness. Permissive parents tend to lack firmness. Assess which distortion of biblical training you would tend toward. Strive for greater balance.

─────── *Application Questions for Chapter 11* ───────

1. What is the problem in your children that requires the use of the rod?

2. What is the function of the rod?

3. Whom has God authorized to discipline children with the rod?

4. Review the common objections to the rod. Have any of these been your objection?

5. Name several distortions of the rod.

6. How would you describe the relationship between communication and the rod? Which method is easier for you?

Embracing Biblical Methods: Appeal to the Conscience

*I*T WASN'T A FAST-PACED program. Perhaps that is why it caught my eye. It was late and my day had been fast-paced enough for me! I had no appetite for the melodrama of someone else's life. The man on the TV spoke flatly. In a gently monotonous voice he explained his craft. He was a painter. I came in while he was preparing the canvas.

"You can't just begin painting," he droned. Before the color, before the texture, before the hues and activity of the painting, the artist puts a wash on the canvas. The wash is the background for all the activity of the painting. The art presupposes the wash.

This chapter is such a wash. The past several chapters discussed communication and the rod. Two issues—appeal to the conscience and focusing on God's redemptive work—have been implied in our consideration of communication and the rod. These issues give biblical shape and structure to our parenting.

Appealing to the Conscience

Your correction and discipline must find their mark in the conscience of your son or daughter. God has given children a reasoning capacity that distinguishes issues of right and wrong. Paul reminds us that even those who do not have the law of God show that its requirements are written on their hearts when they obey the law (Romans 2:12–16). They either excuse or accuse themselves in their thoughts because of their conscience.

This God-given conscience is your ally in discipline and correction. Your most powerful appeals will be those that smite the conscience. When the offended conscience is aroused, correction and discipline can find their mark.

Two biblical illustrations elucidate this issue. Proverbs 23 justifies the use of the rod in correction. Verses 13 and 14 read: "Do not withhold discipline from a child; if you punish him with the rod, he will not die. Punish him with the rod and save his soul from death." The rod, however, is not the only instrument of training in the passage. There is another. It is appeal to the conscience. Earnest entreaty fills this chapter of Proverbs:

> "Don't let your heart envy sinners . . . " (v. 17).
> ". . . keep your heart on the right path . . . " (v. 19).
> "Listen to your father, who gave you life . . . " (v. 22).
> "Buy the truth and do not sell it; get wisdom, discipline and understanding" (v. 23).
> "My son, give me your heart . . ." (v. 26).

The passage actually drips with sweet and tender entreaty that appeals to the conscience. Is Solomon soft on the rod? No! But he realizes the limitation of the rod. He knows that the rod gets the attention, but the conscience must be plowed up and planted with the truth of God's ways.

Jesus' interaction with the Pharisees provides another graphic example of appeal to the conscience. In Matthew 21:23, the chief priests and the elders challenge Christ's authority. He responds with the parable of the two sons:

> *"What do you think? There was a man who had two sons. He went to the first and said, 'Son, go and work today in the vineyard.'*
>
> *" 'I will not,' he answered, but later he changed his mind and went.*
>
> *"Then the father went to the other son and said the same thing. He answered, 'I will, sir,' but he did not go.*
>
> *"Which of the two did what his father wanted?"*
>
> *"The first," they answered.*
>
> *Jesus said to them, "I tell you the truth, the tax collectors and the prostitutes are entering the kingdom of God ahead of you. For John came to you to show you the way of righteousness, and you did not believe him, but the tax collectors and the prostitutes did. And even after you saw this, you did not repent and believe him."* (Matthew 21:28–32)

At the end of the parable he asks them a question that is directed to their reasoning about right and wrong. They answer correctly.

He gives them another parable—the parable of the tenants and vineyard owner:

> *"Listen to another parable: There was a landowner who planted a vineyard. He put a wall around it, dug a winepress in it and built a watchtower. Then he rented the vineyard to some farmers and went away on a journey. When the harvest time approached, he sent his servants to the tenants to collect his fruit.*
>
> *"The tenants seized his servants; they beat one, killed another, and stoned a third. Then he sent other servants to them, more than the first time, and the tenants treated them the same way. Last of all, he sent his son to them. 'They will respect my son,' he said.*
>
> *"But when the tenants saw the son, they said to each other, 'This is the heir. Come, let's kill him and take his inheritance.' So they took him and threw him out of the vineyard and killed him.*
>
> *"Therefore, when the owner of the vineyard comes, what will he do to those tenants?"*

"He will bring those wretches to a wretched end," they replied, "and he will rent the vineyard to other tenants, who will give him his share of the crop at harvest time."

Jesus said to them, "Have you never read in the Scriptures: 'The stone that the builders rejected has become the capstone; the Lord has done this, and it is marvelous in our eyes?'

"Therefore I tell you that the kingdom of God will be taken away from you and given to a people who will produce its fruit. He who falls on this stone will be broken to pieces, but he on whom it falls will be crushed."

When the chief priests and the Pharisees heard Jesus' parables, they knew he was talking about them. They looked for a way to arrest him, but they were afraid of the crowd because the people held that he was a prophet (Matthew 21:33–46).

Note how Jesus appeals to their sense of right and wrong. He is making his appeal to their consciences. "When the owner of the vineyard comes, what will he do?"

He asks them to make a judgment. They judge correctly. Then he shows them that they have indicted themselves. Verse 45 shows that they got the point; Matthew says, "they knew that he was talking about them. . . ."

Here is the pattern. Christ appeals to their conscience so they cannot escape the implications of their sin. Thus, he deals with the root problems, not just the surface issues.

Their original question in Matthew 21:23, "By what authority are you doing these things and who gave you this authority?" sounded like a question about the source of his authority. It was, however, a challenge to his authority. His answer drew the battle lines. He asserted that his authority was from God. While they did not repent, the challenge to the conscience made its mark. They knew he was talking about them. They had indicted themselves.

This is your task in shepherding your children. You must make a point of appealing to the conscience. To see them deal with the issues of their Godward orientation, you must take correction beyond behavior to addressing the issues of the heart. You address the heart by exposing sin and appealing to the conscience as the God-given adjudicator of right and wrong.

Recently, after a worship service, a man approached me in a state of great agitation. He had observed a young boy stealing some money from the offering plate after the church service. He felt genuine concern for the boy. I suggested that he tell the boy's father so that the child could benefit from his father's correction and intervention.

A few minutes later the boy and his father asked to see me in my study. The child produced $2 and said he had taken it from the offering plate. He was in tears, professing his sorrow and asking for forgiveness.

I began to speak to him. "Charlie, I am so glad that someone saw what you did. What a wonderful mercy of God that you did not get away with this! God has spared you the hardness of heart that comes when we sin and get by with it. Don't you see how gracious he has been to you?" He looked me in the eye and nodded.

"You know, Charlie," I continued, "this is why Jesus came. Jesus came because people like you and your father and me have hearts that want to steal. You see, we are so bold and brazen that we would even steal from the offerings that people have given to God. But God had such love for wicked boys and men that he sent his Son to change them from the inside out and make them people who are givers and not takers."

At this point, Charlie broke down in sobs and drew another $20 from his pocket. He had begun this brief conversation prepared to go through the motions and give back two of the dollars he had taken. Something happened as he heard me speak of the mercy of God to wicked sinners. There was no accusation in my tone. Neither his father nor I knew there was more money. What happened? Charlie's conscience was smitten by the gospel! Something in what I said struck a chord that resonated within his young, larcenous heart. The gospel hit its mark in his conscience.

Correcting with a Central Focus on Redemption

The central focus of childrearing is to bring children to a sober assessment of themselves as sinners. They must understand the mercy of God, who offered Christ as a sacrifice for sinners. How is that accomplished? You must address the heart as the fountain of behavior, and the conscience as the God-given judge of right and wrong. The cross of Christ must be the central focus of your childrearing.

You want to see your child live a life that is embedded in the rich soil of Christ's gracious work. The focal point of your discipline and correction must be your children seeing their utter inability to do the things that God requires unless they know the help and strength of God. Your correction must hold the standard of righteousness as high as God holds it. God's standard is correct behavior flowing from a heart that loves God and has God's glory as the sole purpose of life. This is not native to your children (nor to their parents).

Discipline exposes your child's inability to love his sister from his heart, or genuinely to prefer others before himself. Discipline leads to the cross of Christ where sinful people are forgiven. Sinners who come to Jesus in repentance and faith find grace and mercy. Jesus' redemptive work entails forgiveness, internal transformation, and empowerment to live new lives.

The alternative is to reduce the standard to what may be fairly expected of your children without the grace of God. The alternative is to give them a law they can keep. The alternative is a lesser standard that does not require grace and does not cast them on Christ, but rather on their own resources.

Many parents get confused at this point. They realize their children are unable to love others from the heart without salvation and new birth. So they conclude that, since it is not possible, the standard must be lowered. They set a standard that is in keeping with their children's resources.

Dependence on their own resources moves them away from the cross. It moves them away from any self-assessment that would force them to conclude that they desperately need Jesus' forgiveness and power.

I have spoken to many parents who feared they were producing little hypocrites who were proud and self-righteous. Hypocrisy and self-righteousness is the result of giving children a keepable law and telling them to be good. To the extent they are successful, they become like the Pharisees, people whose exterior is clean, while inside they are full of dirt and filth. The genius of Phariseeism was that it reduced the law to a keepable standard of externals that any self-disciplined person could do. In their pride and self-righteousness, they rejected Christ.

Correction and shepherding must focus on Christ. It is only in Christ that the child who has strayed and has experienced conviction of sin may find hope, forgiveness, salvation, and power to live.

Application Questions for Chapter 12

1. To whom does your child feel accountable when he sins?

2. How do you keep your children focused on the fact that obedience to parents is based on God's command? Do you ever find yourself basing your requirements simply on your will and desires?

3. Are you focusing your correction and direction on behavior or on attitudes of the heart? Do your children think of themselves as sinners because of what they do or because of what they are?

4. How is appealing to the conscience different from addressing behavior? What benefits come from appeal to the conscience rather than focusing on behavior?

5. Hope for sinful children is found in Christ. How do you focus hope for your child in the work of Christ?

6. Do you ever find yourself yelling at your kids in such a manner that it would be impossible to stop and pray for Christ to help them?

SHEPHERDING THE
HEART SUMMARIZED

*I*N THE FIRST PART of this book, I have laid out the foundations
for biblical childrearing. This chapter briefly summarizes the
elements of Part One.

1. Your children are the product of two things. The first—shaping
influence—is their physical makeup and their life experience. The
second—Godward orientation—determines how they interact with
that experience. Parenting involves (1) providing the best shaping
influences you can and (2) the careful shepherding of your children's
responses to those influences.

2. The heart determines behavior. Learn, therefore, to work back
from behavior to the heart. Expose heart struggles. Help your children see that they were made for a relationship with God. The thirst
of the heart can be satisfied in truly knowing God.

3. You have authority because God has made you his agent. This
means you are on his errand, not yours. Your task is to help your
children know God and the true nature of reality. This will enable
them to know themselves.

4. Since the chief end of man is to glorify God and enjoy him forever, you must set such a worldview before your children. You must help them learn that only in him will they find themselves.

5. Biblical goals must be accomplished through biblical methods. Therefore, you must reject the substitute methods that our culture presents.

6. God has given two methods for childrearing. They are (1) communication and (2) the rod. These methods must be woven together in your practice. Your children need to be known and understood. Thus, rich communication is necessary. They also need authority and firmness. Thus, the rod is necessary. The rod functions to underscore the importance of the things you talk about with them.

In Part Two we will apply these principles to the specifics of childrearing in the various stages of childhood development.

SHEPHERDING
THROUGH THE STAGES
OF CHILDHOOD

INFANCY TO
CHILDHOOD:
TRAINING OBJECTIVES

*H*OWARD'S SON SUFFERED brain damage during infancy. Howard was unsure how much his son could understand. Despite his son's retarded brain development, he talked to him about the ways of God. At 3½, the boy still could not speak. The parents continued to talk to him of God, pray with him, and sought to shepherd him biblically.

One day, the lad required correction and discipline. Howard was perplexed as he tried to explain, not knowing how much his son could grasp. As he grew more frustrated with the communication process, his son intervened. He spoke! His first words were, "Pray, Daddy!"

This young child, compromised by brain damage, had been understanding valuable lessons all along. He knew of his father's faith in God. He knew that one turns to God when troubled. He knew that God could help his daddy communicate. What an illustration of the importance of these early years!

Primary Characteristic—Change

The first stage of development, infancy to childhood, encompasses the period from birth to age four or five. This period can be described in a single word—change. With every stage of development, the child astounds his parents with dramatic change.

Physical Change

Think of the physical changes. The new infant is immobile. He can't lift his head. He can't roll over. He can't sit. Yet powerful forces are at work in him. In several months he is sitting, standing, toddling, and even walking. He learns to run, hop on one foot, climb trees; to do things you are too decrepit to do anymore.

He develops his capacity to manipulate objects. Soon he can turn doorknobs and release catches. He learns to feed himself. There is no period of life in which physical change is so dramatic.

Social Change

Social change is just as radical. The first social relationship is with his mother. Soon, the circle of familiar people widens to include other family members. He learns his own style of relating to others. He learns what endears him to others. He learns how to seek approval in his ever-widening world of social relationships. By four or five, he will have friends of his own.

Intellectual Change

Intellectual change is just as dramatic. The young child is a meaning maker. He hears language and generalizes the rules of grammar. Even his mistakes follow the logical grammar patterns—"I thinked" instead of "I thought."

Every experience is a learning experience. Curiosity abounds. Why do doors turn on hinges? Do things exist when I don't think about them? Why do things fall to the ground? Can people see me when I close my eyes? The child learns to talk, to count, to tease, to be funny, to be serious. He learns values—what is important and what isn't.

Spiritual Change

He is developing spiritually. That development may be shepherded along the lines of knowing and loving the true God, or it may be ignored. Both produce spiritual development. Because he is a spiritual creature, he either learns to worship and rely on Jehovah God, or he learns to bow before lesser gods.

Summary

The rapid changes during these early years give parents grandiose ideas about their children. Many parents are sure their kindergarten children are geniuses. They have to be; they catch on so well. They have learned so much in such a short period of time. Parents are sure there is no limit to this child's capacity.

Understanding Authority

With such dramatic changes over a short time, it is easy to lose focus. Where should you put your energies? You need a single overarching training objective, narrow enough to give firm direction in concrete situations and broad enough to encompass the changing world of the young child.

One Big Lesson

The most important lesson for the child to learn in this period is that HE IS AN INDIVIDUAL UNDER AUTHORITY. He has been made by God and has a responsibility to obey God in all things.

The key passage of Scripture for this period is:

> *Children obey your parents in the Lord, for this is right.* "Honor your father and mother,"—*which is the first commandment with a promise*—"that it may go well with you and that you may enjoy long life on the earth" (Ephesians 6:1–3).

Godward Focus

Notice that obedience is a response to God. Children must learn that they have been made for God. They have a duty to him. He has the right to rule them. They owe him obedience.

Your children will never submit to you without understanding this truth. They will never see living in terms of bringing glory to God. They will be self-absorbed—the prime objects of worship in their own world.

Submission to earthly authority is a specific application of being a creature under God's authority. Submission to God's authority may seem distant and theoretical. Mom and Dad, however, are present. Obedience to God is reflected in a child's growing understanding of obedience to parents.

Acquaint your children with authority and submission when they are infants. This training starts the day you bring them home from the hospital.

These lessons, firmly established in early years, will yield fruit throughout childhood. Establish these principles and you will eliminate the need to have repeated contests over authority.

With our first teen-age driver, we were concerned about the car becoming a social environment that was outside parental control. We established clear guidelines. There were rules against having passengers who had not been approved by Mom and Dad. There were also rules against changes in destination. We, of course, welcomed phone calls of appeal. Plans can always change; we just didn't want any surprises. We were pleased to get occasional calls to change arrangements and to learn of many times when our son did not take passengers or make runs that had not been approved in advance. He could have done so without our knowledge, but he didn't. We had a teen driver we could trust because of the lessons learned in early childhood.

Circle of Blessing

In Ephcsians 6:1–3, God has drawn a circle of great blessing. Children are to live within the circle of submission to parental authority.

Submission to parents means HONORING and OBEYING. Within that circle things will go well and they will enjoy long lives.

Things Go Well

It is imperative that children learn to honor and obey. It will go well with them. Their obedience is not secured so that you can be obeyed for your sake. You must be obeyed for their sakes! They are the direct beneficiaries of honoring and obeying Mom and Dad. The disobedient child has moved outside the circle of blessing. The parent must quickly restore the child to the proper relationship with God and the parent. As the child returns to the circle of blessing, things go well for him. He enjoys long life.

Figure 7 Circle of Safety

Safety Rather Than Danger

The circle of submission to parental authority is the place of safety. By implication, being outside that circle is a place of danger; it will not go well with him and he will not enjoy a long life.

Your child is in danger if he is rebellious and disobedient. You, therefore, must move swiftly to return him to the circle of protection and safety.

The Rescue Function

The function of the rod and communication is rescue. Correction and discipline moves your child from the peril of rebellion and disobedience back into the circle of safety. The child has not just disobeyed Mommy or Daddy. He has disobeyed God. He has made himself liable to the discipline and correction that God has appointed for disobedient children. The function of discipline is to restore him to the safety and protection of the circle.

I have drawn this circle for my children scores of times, entreating them to willing submission to authority, explaining that Dad was not mad at them, but rather Dad was on a rescue mission. I have asked them, "How could I see you in peril and not seek to rescue you?"

Honoring Defined

Honoring parents means to treat them with respect and esteem because of their position of authority. It is honoring them because of their role of authority. If a child is going to honor his parents, it will be the result of two things: 1) The parent must train him to do so. 2) The parent must be honorable in his conduct and demeanor.

It is not easy to train children to honor parents in a culture in which no one is honored. One of the clearest ways to show honor is in the way children speak to their parents. Children must never speak to their parents in imperatives. They must never speak to Mom and Dad as they would speak to a peer. They must be taught to express their thoughts in a manner that shows proper respect.

This can be done kindly through statements such as these: "I am sorry, dear, but you may not speak to me in that way. God has made me your mother and has said that you must treat me with honor. Now, let's see if there is a respectful way you can express what you wish to say."

Or, "Dear, I am not one of your chums. You may speak to your friends in a flippant manner, but you may not speak to me in that way. Now, what was it that you wanted to say?" Or, "Dear, you cannot give me orders. You may make requests, but you cannot give me orders because God has made me the authority over you."

Do not wait for this training until your children are teenagers. If you do, you will suffer the indignity of their disrespect. Deal with this in the first several years. Respectful teenagers are developed when they are 1, 2, 3, 4, or 5, not at 13, 14, 15, or 16. (If you find yourself confronted with disrespectful teens, get these concepts under your belt and talk with them about how you should have raised them.)

I observed a recent conversation:

PARENT: Dear, I want you to sit down now.
CHILD: [With an impudent grin] Why?
PARENT: I think that you need to slow down a little.
CHILD: [Same grin, a little taunting] Why?
PARENT: Because . . .
CHILD: Why?
PARENT: Because . . .
CHILD: Why?
PARENT: Because . . .
CHILD: Why?

After a few minutes, the mother of this child turned toward me in explanation. "Sometimes I just can't get him to be serious."

This lad was being serious. He knew that his mother wanted cooperation. He was not about to submit to her. Things could not have been more serious.

A parent who is respectful to his children and teaches them with dignity and respect will be respected by his children. You may not yell at your children. You do not make them your slaves. Suffering indignities from you cannot be a part of submission to authority. When you fail to be respectful or courteous, or sin against them, you must seek forgiveness. There is a sowing and reaping principle here. Whatever you sow you shall reap. It is as true in childrearing as it is anywhere.

Obedience Defined

Obedience is out of vogue in our culture. You can find classes that provide assertiveness training, but try to find classes in submissiveness training! Obedience is the willing submission of one person to the authority of another. It means more than a child doing what he is told. It means doing what he is told—

>*Without Challenge*
>*Without Excuse*
>*Without Delay*

Often, submission means doing what he doesn't want to do, at least what he doesn't want to do at that moment.

If you rouse your children and announce that you are taking them to an amusement park for the day, you would not regard their cooperation as submission. They are doing what they want. It may be done at the suggestion of their father, but it is not submission, because it is something they wanted to do. My point is this: Submission to authority means that your child will have to do things that he does not wish to do.

You inevitably train your children in obedience. You may train them to obey only after you've yelled, pleaded, or threatened. You may train them to obey only when they wish to. You may not train them to obey at all. Even that is a type of training in obedience.

When your directives are met by a discourse about why what you have asked is not fair, your children are not obeying. When you are met with excuses or explanations, they are not obeying. When they refuse to respond at once, they are not obeying. Submission to authority means that they obey without delay, excuse, or challenge.

It is easy to think unclearly about obedience. When you say to your child, "Dear, I want you to go to bed now," there is only one appropriate response. It is not, "I'll go after I finish coloring this page." It is not, "Why do I always have to go to bed so early?" It is not to ignore you entirely.

There is only one obedient response. It is to go to bed without delay. If you accept any other response, you are training your children to disobey.

Remember what is at stake; that it go well with your children and that they enjoy a long life. They must honor and obey.

Call for Consistency

The serious parent must be prepared to swim upstream, as our culture has lost any semblance of submission to authority. You must be consistent. You must train your children to obey through careful discipline and precise instruction. The rules have to be the same each day.

If they must obey, you must challenge disobedience and persevere until the lessons of submission are learned. Victory does not come to the faint of heart. You will rarely witness resolute will power such as you find in a toddler who has determined not to obey.

Clear directives and thorough reinforcement are essential. Never allow your children to disobey without dealing with them. When they disobey, they are moving out of the circle of God's blessing into a place of grave peril. If you understand the fear of the Lord, you will not allow your child to ignore God's law without intervening. Your intervention is turning him back into the circle of blessing.

Some parents argue, "It is a glory to overlook an offense," as a justification for allowing some disobedience. They do not understand the issue. Obedience to parents is not a parent-child issue. If it were, the parent could be selective about when he wished to be obeyed. Obedience is not simply an issue between the parent and the child. It is an issue between the child and God in which the parent is God's agent in drawing the child back within the circle of blessing. It is not a glory to overlook offenses of that sort.

Once the lessons of submission are learned, they are learned for a lifetime! As I write, my children are in high school and college. We have not had a contest over the issue of submission for years. God is faithful to his promise.

Process of Appeal

Once your children understand that they are creatures under authority and that they cannot always do what they like, you can begin to teach them how to appeal to their authorities.

You cannot accept refusal to obey. You cannot accept obedience only when your children are convinced you are right or fair. You cannot be required to sell them on the propriety of your directives. These issues must be firmly in place. They are non-negotiables.

You can, however, teach them to appeal to authority. They are not machines. They have ideas and thoughts. Daniel 1 shows us how to appeal to authorities. It is important to teach your children how to appeal in a respectful manner.

The appeal process is a safety valve for the biblical requirement of obedience. It is a safety check in two directions. 1) It is a check against caprice on your part. Perhaps you have spoken quickly without careful thought. Appeal provides a context for you to rescind a directive that was spoken in haste or was inappropriate. 2) It is a safety valve for your children. They know that they have permission to appeal a directive. They know that Mom and Dad will honestly reconsider and will rescind the directive if that is good for the individual or family. This keeps the kids from feeling they "can't fight city hall." The appeal procedure is a good "after-command" safety valve.

There is an important "before-command" safety valve for parents. The wise parent will weigh whether the directive he is giving is necessary and appropriate.

For example, imagine your child is reading in bed. It is time for lights out. You could simply throw the switch. You could tell him to shut off the lights. Either way, the child's duty is to obey. Or you could ask, "How many pages to the end of that chapter? Oh, only a page and a half. Okay, you may finish and then turn off the lights." As a wise parent, you must exercise sensitivity to your child's needs and wishes as you provide direction. By doing so, you model godly authority that is truly kind.

Pattern for Appeal

Here are some important guidelines to follow in making a biblical appeal.

1) You begin to obey immediately, not after appeal.
2) You must be prepared to obey either way.
3) You must appeal in a respectful manner.
4) You must accept the result of the appeal with a gracious spirit.

Illustration of Appeal

Mother says, "It is time to go to bed." The child begins to head for bed, and while en route may ask, "Is it okay if I finish coloring this picture first?" Mother may say, "Yes, that would be okay," or she may say "No, dear, you were up late last night. You need your sleep." Whichever the answer, the child must be prepared to obey without challenge, without excuse, without delay.

It should be our habit to say "Yes" to a request unless there are good reasons to say "No". It is easy to say "No" because we do not want to think through the implications of saying "Yes."

The benefits of this appeal procedure are obvious. The child has some recourse. He learns to submit to authority in a context that is not arbitrary. He learns to approach his superiors in a respectful manner. The parent can change his mind in the context of respectful appeal, but not in the presence of blatant rebellion.

The Importance of Example

It is so difficult to teach submission to authority in a culture in which we have few models to follow. At one time, adults provided examples of submission to authority. Mom submitted to Dad as the head of the house. Dad submitted to his boss. There was a general concept of one's station in life and behaving in the manner appropriate to it.

Various liberation movements in the second half of the 20th century have changed all that. Since our culture's interest in the equality and dignity of individuals is not rooted in Scripture, we have lost the idea of respect for a person because of his or her office or place of authority. Therefore, our children are growing up in a culture with no ready models of submission to authority.

You must provide examples of submission for your children. Dads can model this by exercising gracious, biblical authority over family life, and Moms through biblical submission to their husbands. It can be done through biblical submission to employers. It can be shown through your relationship to the state and the church. Ensure that your interaction with various authorities are examples of submission.

The way you respond to disappointment with your authorities in the society, at the job, and in the church, teaches your children how to be under authority. The attitudes you display teach either biblical submission or unbiblical independence and rebellion.

Shepherding Your Children in Godly Attitudes

A primary concern of this book is the Godward orientation of your children. Shepherding that relationship is one of the primary tasks of parenting.

Teaching to submit to authority presents you with beautiful opportunities to shepherd your child's relationship to God. God commands children to obey Mom and Dad. That is God's directive. Your children must be brought to see that living in God's world as creatures means submission to that good and wise God in all things. The call to submit to Mommy and Daddy is a call to trust God rather than "self." "Self" tells your child not to submit. "Self" says, "Do what you want, when you want, and how you want."

What a wonderful opportunity to talk to children about the rebellion of their hearts! Show them how they are inclined to disobey and turn irrationally from what is good for them. Confront them with their weakness and inability to obey God without God's work within. What happens to the child who becomes persuaded that obedience is good for him? Do his problems with submission melt away? No, no more than yours do when you know what you should do. Doing what he knows is good may still elude him. This, too, takes him to God. He must learn to get hold of God for help and strength to obey.

The gospel seems irrelevant to the smug child who isn't required to do anything he does not want to do. It seems irrelevant to the arrogant child who has been told all his life how wonderful he is. But the gospel has great relevance for the child who is persuaded that God calls him to do something that is not native to his sinful heart—to joyfully and willingly submit to the authority of someone else! Only the power of the gospel can give a willing heart and the strength to obey.

Benefits of Learning to be Under Authority

God has promised that children who honor and obey will have things go well for them and will enjoy long life on the earth. Obviously, the child who submits to parental authority is richly blessed. I grieve to see children who were never taught these principles knocked about by life because of their rebellious, unsubmissive behavior. By contrast, I delight to see parents internalize these principles and raise their children with a healthy respect for and submission to authority. The result is children for whom it does go well. They are respected by their teachers. They are given special opportunities. They are esteemed by their peers in the Christian community. They grow in spiritual insight as they submit to God and walk in wisdom's path. Genuine submission to godly authority bears good fruit.

The child trained in biblical obedience is better able to understand the gospel. The power and grace of the gospel is most deeply understood, not by those who never face their biblical duties, but by those who do. Knowing our native resistance to authority, knowing our inability to do what God has commanded, we are confronted with our need for the grace and power of Jesus Christ. Paul's prayer that God would work by his Spirit in the inner man in great power takes on relevance. It is only that power that can get your children back to the circle in which God protects and blesses.

What are the secondary lessons of biblical discipline? Even though the child will not be able to fully appreciate the importance of submission, training him to do what he ought, regardless of how he feels, prepares him to be a person who lives by principle rather than mood or impulse. He learns that he cannot trust himself to judge right and wrong. He must have a reference point outside himself. He learns that behavior has moral implications and inevitable outcomes.

Save Time—Do It Right

One winter, work was scarce. As a contractor, the only work I could find was putting in a basement. The problem was that the house had already been built. I spent the winter with a crew excavating and pouring walls and floors. We actually built a basement under the existing house. It was valuable lakefront property, so the investment was worthwhile. But I can testify that it is better to build the foundation before you build the house!

This issue—submission to authority—is foundational for the entire parent-child relationship. It is possible to build this foundation after the house has been started. It is, however, more difficult and more expensive.

If your children are young, do it right from the start. Don't let them develop habits of disobedience. Be sure that they learn to obey without challenge, without excuse, without delay.

If your children are older your task will be a little more difficult. Begin with gracious and kind instruction. Take them to passages like Ephesians 6; help them see the logic and wisdom of being a person under authority, Your goal is to persuade them that even though submission is hard, it is the path of blessing and peace.

Don't waste time trying to sugarcoat submission to make it palatable. Submission necessarily means doing what you do not wish to do. It is never easy or painless. True biblical submission must be found in knowing Christ and his grace. Don't try to make it something that does not require grace. Don't reduce submission to authority to that which fits natural man and natural abilities.

We will next look at the training procedures used for children in this period from infancy to childhood.

——— *Application Questions for Chapter 14* ———

1. Why is obedience the best thing for your child?

2. What promises does God make to those who honor and obey parents?

3. What guidelines should you establish to implement biblical authority?

4. How can you speak to your school-age children about changing your home from being a home with problems to a properly ordered home?

5. Why is giving room for appeal so important in the parenting process?

6. What dangers must be avoided in the appeal process?

7. Are you a good model of submission to authorities?

8. What are the patterns of disobedience you have tolerated in your home?

9. What are the patterns of disrespect you have tolerated in your home?

10. What areas do you need to clarify to establish authority in your home?

11. What are the negative effects of your failure to establish biblical authority?

12. What promises of Scripture encourage you to establish authority in your home?

13. Could you reproduce and explain Figure 7?

15

INFANCY
TO CHILDHOOD:
TRAINING
PROCEDURES

W̶E USED TO OBSERVE cyclical patterns in the behavior of our children. Every few months, they would become unruly. They weren't in actual rebellion, but their obedience was sluggish. There was a growing delay between receiving our direction and responding.

We would redouble our efforts. We would be more precise in giving direction. We would be more consistent about discipline. We would quit reminding, pleading, and snapping. We would return to basics—speaking once and expecting obedience—disciplining if obedience was not forthcoming.

Overnight, our home would become peaceful again. The children would be happy and obedient. We would be more patient. We would feel more successful as parents.

One day it dawned on us! We produced the cycles. When things went well, we became lax. Eventually, the deterioration in our children's behavior would become painfully obvious. We would respond with renewed courage and effort.

In order to teach your children to be under authority, you must be prepared to discipline disobedience. Consistency is mandated if your children are to learn that God requires obedience.

Disobedience coupled with failure to discipline sends mixed messages. On the one hand, you say they must obey. You tell them that temporal and eternal well-being is attached to obedience. On the other hand, you accept disobedience and tolerate behavior that places them at risk.

Recall with me the chart from the last chapter. In Ephesians 6:1–3, God's ways form a circle of submission to parental authority.

Submission to parents means honoring and obeying. Within that circle is blessing and long life. As soon as your child steps out of that circle of safety, he needs to be rescued from the danger of stubborn independence from your authority. Your authority represents God's authority. (Remember, you function as agents of God.) The

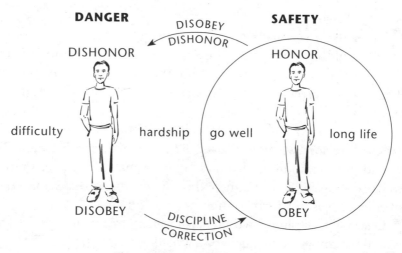

Figure 8 Rescue from Danger

rescue squad is Mom or Dad, armed with the methods God has given—namely the rod and communication.

In these early years of childhood, the rod is primary. It is primary because God has commanded it. Remember, God says that "Folly is bound up in the heart of a child, but the rod of discipline will drive it far from him" (Proverbs 22:15).

A young child does not give proper weight to words alone. His attention is secured when those words are punctuated by a sound spanking.

The "When" of Spanking

When does a child need a spanking? When you have given a directive that he has heard and is within his capacity to understand, and he has not obeyed without challenge, without excuse or without delay, he needs a spanking. If you fail to spank, you fail to take God's Word seriously. You are saying you do not believe what the Bible teaches about the import of these issues. You are saying that you do not love your child enough to do the painful things that God has called you to.

The "when" of spanking is so simple that parents miss it. If your child has not obeyed, he needs to be spanked. If he has failed to respond to your direction, he has moved out of the circle of safety.

If obedience is to be absolutely mandatory for him, you cannot ignore or overlook disobedience. If disobedience is okay sometimes, then why not at all times?

Failure to be consistent is capricious. Inconsistency means that correction revolves around your convenience rather than around objective biblical principle. While they are still young, you must teach your children that obedience is a necessity, not one of many options.

If you accept challenge, delay, or excuses, you are not training in submission. You are, rather, training your children how to manipulate authorities and live on the ragged edge of disobedience.

You teach them to toss you an occasional bone of obedience to keep you at bay.

You must not warn. You must not ask if they want to be spanked. If you do, you are training them to wait for the warning before they obey. Your children must understand that when you speak for the first time, you have spoken for the last time.

Sometimes, the challenge to God's authority (mediated through you as his agent) is not just failure to obey. Sometimes it is verbal. Perhaps the child says "No" to your request. Perhaps you receive a whining "Why?" Perhaps you receive a look of disgust and disdain. Whatever form it takes, rebellion must be challenged. Remember, the issue at stake is your child's good. Your disobedient child has moved out of the context of blessing—submission to parental authority.

We could think of it like this. The child who is disobedient is living as a fool. "The fool says in his heart, 'There is no God.'" The fool is one who says, "I refuse to acknowledge that there is a God, to whom I am accountable." Such a stance is pure folly, from which you must rescue your child with all due haste.

The "How" of Spanking

How do you go about giving a spanking? There are many problems to avoid. You must avoid responding in anger. You must avoid treating your child without proper respect for his person and dignity. You must temper unwavering firmness with kindness and gentleness. Remember that discipline is a rescue mission. You must keep the spanking focused on issues of the heart.

The following procedure can provide discipline that preserves the child's dignity:

1. Take your child to a private place where he can be spoken with in privacy. Discipline must not rob a child of his dignity. You should never discipline in front of the other children in the family; it is not a spectator activity. The object is not to humiliate the child. You show respect for him by giving him privacy.

2. Tell him specifically what he has done or failed to do. Physical discipline must be attached to specific, easily demonstrated issues. As your child's conceptual understanding grows, you may sometimes correct for more general, attitudinal issues, but not with pre-school children. Your spankings must always be issue-oriented. The spanking should always address a specific attitude or incident. Never spank just for "general purposes" or because you've "had it."

3. Secure an acknowledgment from the child of what he has done. This will often take some time. Many times children will want to avoid the spanking badly enough to lie about what they have done.

The conversation may go like this:

FATHER: Daddy told you that you should pick up your toys, didn't he?
CHILD: [child nodding] Yes.
FATHER: You didn't obey me, did you?
CHILD: [looking down] No.
FATHER: You know what Daddy must do. He must spank you. . . .

The child has acknowledged what he has done. This ensures that he knows why he is being spanked.

4. Remind him that the function of the spanking is not venting your frustration or because you are angry, but to restore him to the place in which God has promised blessing. Express your concern that he has removed himself from the place of proper submission to your authority. The spanking must reflect your obedience to God's directives and concern for the child's good. You have no right to hit your child under any circumstance other than biblically sanctioned discipline.

5. Tell the child how many swats he will receive. (This is an important signal that you are in control of yourself.) The number of swats will vary with different children. One of our sons had a leather bottom. He was not easily impressed. We had another

son who was so compliant that he obeyed as soon as he saw the paddle. He required less.

6. Remove his drawers so that the spanking is not lost in the padding of his pants. This should be done at the last possible moment. They should be returned as soon as you are done. It is best to lay the child across your lap rather than over a bed or a chair. This puts the spanking in the context of your physical relationship. He is not being removed from you to a neutral object for the purpose of being disciplined.

As children get older and more self-conscious you must be careful not to shame or embarrass them. Here is a good rule of thumb. If you child is young enough that you care for his hygiene, it will not embarrass him if you see his bottom during a spanking. You see his bottom every day in the course of ordinary business. If he is old enough that he is in charge of his own hygiene (he bathes himself, changes his own underclothes and so forth) then leave his underpants on. You don't want to embarrass your child or make them feel the shame of nakedness. You just want to be sure there are no comic books stuffed into the pants that would keep you from being effective.

7. After you have spanked, take the child up on your lap and hug him, telling him how much you love him, how much it grieves you to spank him, and how you hope that it will not be necessary again. This keeps the spanking referenced to restoration, not retribution.

At this point there should be complete restoration between you and your child. If he will not be restored to you, if he is mad at you, if he refuses to receive your affection, then something is wrong. In such cases, check two things.

Check your own spirit. Have you handled him roughly? Have you been out of control? Have you sinned against him in the way you have disciplined? If you have brought unholy anger on this holy mission, you must confess your sin and seek forgiveness and restoration.

Check his spirit. Is his anger a reflection of rejection of your discipline? Is he mad at you? Is he trying to punish you for what you have done? If so, the discipline session is not over.

We have always been guided by Hebrews 12:11: "No discipline seems pleasant at the time, but painful. Later on, however, it produces a harvest of righteousness and peace for those who have been trained by it." If discipline has not yielded a harvest of peace and righteousness, it is not finished. On some occasions I have had to say to our children: "Dear, Daddy has spanked you, but you are not sweet enough yet. We are going to have to go back upstairs for another spanking."

Clearly, I am not going to repeat the entire spanking over and over if the child is not willing to be restored. But if the discipline session has not yielded the harvest of peace, I must signal to the child that something is radically wrong. I might say something like this: "I love you, son, I have disciplined you as much as is appropriate at this time. My desire is to see you submit to Daddy. My goal is total restoration of our relationship and closeness. I am going to pray for us. I am going to pray that I will be a dad who is wise and kind. I will pray that you will submit to God's order for family life and will honor and obey Mom and Dad.

This restoration process is paramount. If the issue has not been your personal anger, but the child's moving out of the circle of safety, then you don't want your child to be in the doghouse. Nor do you want to be in the doghouse.

When the discipline is over, it is over. There is no carryover. The slate is clean. It is time to start fresh. The restoration process ensures that you can do that.

8. Pray with him. Encourage him with the fact that Christ is given because we are people who sin. There is forgiveness in Christ. Christ can be known. Christ can remove his heart of stone and give a heart of flesh. Christ can work by his Spirit to compel him to obey God. Christ can empower and enable him to obey in the future.

You need to shepherd your children in the ways of God at all times. There is, however, no more powerful time to press the claims of the gospel than when your children are being confronted with their need of Christ's grace and power during discipline. When the wax is soft during discipline, the time is right to impress the glories of Christ's redemption.

In terms of training methods, you are using both the processes God has given: the rod and communication. Because you are dealing with young children, there is a heavy emphasis on the undeniably tactile experience of spanking. Your words have weight with a young child if they are underscored with a spanking.

Recall Chapter 7, "Discarding Unbiblical Methods." You will either correct and discipline using the means of the rod and communication, or you will inevitably fall back on one of the methods we rejected in Chapter 7. Some parents succumb to bribing, making contracts, using behavior modification, making heavy emotional appeals, grounding their children, etc. There are no parents that do not train. All parents train in some way. The problem is that much of it is poor training.

The "Why" of Spanking

The "why" is that God commands it. Additionally, spanking enables you to deal with issues of the heart. Remember, the heart directs behavior. Discipline addresses the heart. It does not focus on behavior alone.

Bad behavior represents a failure to obey and is, therefore, the occasion for correction—but the focal point of correction is not behavior. The focal point is the heart of the child that is called to submission to God's authority. The goal of correction is not simply to modify behavior, but to bring the child to sweet, harmonious, and humble heart submission to God's will that he obey Mom and Dad. The heart is the battleground. The spanking comes only because it is God's method of driving foolishness far from your child's heart.

While you have an eye on the here and now, you know that there is more at stake. Where will your child be 30 years from now if no one ever challenges his determination to do whatever he wants whenever he wants? What kind of husband will he be if he refuses to submit to God's rule? What kind of employee will he be if he never learns to submit to authority?

Where will your grandchildren be 50 years from now if the foolishness bound up in your child's heart is never driven away? How will your child ever see his need of Christ's forgiveness and grace if he never faces the native rebellion of his nature and his inability to obey God from the heart?

Frequently Asked Questions

As I have taught in many places around the world about shepherding toddlers, the following questions are often asked.

What is a Spanking Issue?

In this stage when you are teaching children to be people under authority, spanking should be reserved for issues of defiance—failure to honor and failure to obey. When dealing with a toddler, it is less important that he remember the house rules. You should be willing to tell him every time you place him in the highchair that he cannot throw his food on the floor. You certainly don't want to discipline for childishness. Children are clumsy and they lack mature judgment. They are going to knock things over and break them. Accidents due to clumsiness are not an occasion to spank.

With young children you must keep the focus very crisp; spank only for defiance. As children get older, it is fair to have some issues that are house rules. If you do not allow sliding down the bannister or leaping from the bannister to the sofa, it is fair to expect a school-age child to remember such things. It would be appropriate to deal with that as a spanking-for-disobedience issue.

When Is My Child Old Enough?

When your child is old enough to resist your directives, he is old enough to be disciplined. When he is resisting you, he is disobeying. If you fail to respond, those rebellious responses become entrenched. The longer you put off disciplining, the more intractable the disobedience will become.

Rebellion can be something as simple as a small child struggling against a diaper change or stiffening his body when you want him to sit on your lap. The discipline procedure is the same as that which is laid out above. You have no way of knowing how much a child less than a year old can understand, but we do know that understanding comes long before the ability to articulate.

Your temptation will be to wait until your children are speaking and able to articulate their rebellion before you deal with it. When our oldest child was approximately 8 months old, we were confronted with parenting our first mobile child. He crawled everywhere. We had a bookshelf constructed of boards and bricks. Fearing the shelf would fall on him, Margy told him not to pull himself up by the shelf. After moving him away from the shelf, she left the room. As she peeked in on him, she observed him surveying the room. Not seeing her, he headed back toward the forbidden bookshelf. Here was a young child, not yet able to walk or to talk, looking to see if the coast was clear so he could disobey. Obviously, he was old enough to be disciplined.

When is a Child Too Old?

I always tell parents that I do not know the answer to this question; there are so many variables to take into account. There are maturational differences between children. There is the place of a child within the constellation of other children in your home. There are differences in disposition and temperament. All of this makes it both impossible and unwise to create an arbitrary date after which one would never spank.

What I find is this. Spanking is most effective in dealing with young children. They fear being spanked. The spanking gives weight to your words. The spanking sobers and humbles the child. As children get older they get more stoic about spanking. They learn how to deal with it. The intensity of spanking required to make the same impression on a 12-year-old that you make on a 2-year-old would be excessive.

As children mature, there are other consequences to be employed. In a later chapter we will examine means and methods to employ when dealing with older children and teens.

Can I Use Time-Out Instead of Spanking?

Many times in discussions after teaching about spanking I have had conversations that go something like this: "Tedd, I love all the stuff you are teaching, the circle of blessing, the emphasis on the grace of the gospel, the importance of communication; it's all great. But here's the deal, I don't like spanking; can't I use time-outs instead?"

You do not have the right to substitute what God has commanded with the popular ideas of the culture. God calls parents to spank their children. As a parent you do not have the right to say, "I don't like God's idea; I like my idea or the culture's plan better."

You need to trust God and obey God. That said, if you have a rambunctious 2-year-old, it may be appropriate to say "Here, honey, you need to sit for a minute and calm down. Here is a book you can look at; I'll let you know when you are allowed to get up." Or if something ugly has transpired, to say to your 8-year-old, "You need to go to your room and think about what you said, or what you did. I will come and speak with you later." Neither of these are wrong things to do, but you cannot substitute time-out for spanking.

What If My Child Says, "But I Didn't Hear You"?

I have never challenged the validity of this statement, but I have taught my children that it was not acceptable. One of our children seemed to have much trouble with "hearing."

We sat down with this child and had this conversation: "You are having trouble hearing. I am speaking to you in normal conversational tones. I am in close enough proximity for you to hear me. I think, therefore, that you better start to develop the ability to pick my voice out of the other noise in your world. When you hear my voice, you should perk up your ears. From now on, if you fail to obey because you 'did not hear', I will spank you for failing to listen to my voice."

We only had one spanking for failure to hear. After that the hearing problem cleared up.

If I Follow Your Counsel, All I'll Do Is Spank

It often seems to parents that such exactness regarding obedience is asking too much of them and their children. The truth is, if parents are consistent with discipline, they will find quickly that the child responds and the necessity for discipline decreases.

Could it be that you are confronted with disobedience all day because you tolerate it? As long as you are unwilling to require precision in obedience you will have sloppy responses to your directives. Consistency is the key.

There are long-term issues at stake. It is possible to get over the obedience hurdle before your children are school-age. I pity parents who spend their entire lives in contests over obeying, when authority can be settled early in childhood.

There may be days in which nothing much gets done because of the demands of consistent discipline. But, faithfulness will yield a good harvest. It is possible to get beyond the authority issue. Basic obedience does not have to be an issue in your home if you deal with it in these early years. Consistency will enable you to avoid obedience contests throughout your child's life. It is possible to put this problem behind you.

What If I'm Too Mad?

Every parent has felt blinding rage toward a misbehaving child. This is a clear indicator that you are in no position to engage in biblical discipline. When you are in a rage, you are not considering issues of biblical correction. Your agenda is satisfying your own sense of justice. If you're not careful, you will pollute the process of discipline with your unholy anger.

If you are a person who struggles with anger, you know it. If you think you may be near a borderline, ask your spouse to handle any required spanking. If you have a low flashpoint you must promise your children and your spouse: "I will never spank until I have gotten alone with God to quiet my heart so that I can discipline in godly and gracious ways."

If you are too mad to discipline properly, instruct your child to take a seat or go to his room. Then you must seek the face of God. You must repent of your anger. You must remain before God until you are able to deal with your child in integrity.

If, in the weakness and frailty of your flesh, you sin against your children, you must seek their forgiveness. Seeking forgiveness is not saying, "I am sorry that I got mad at you and yelled, but when you do that. . . ." Seeking forgiveness is saying, "I am sorry. I sinned against you. I was mad. I threw a temper fit. There is no justification for behavior like that. Please forgive me." When you give reasons for your sin, you are not asking forgiveness, you are simply justifying your sin.

What If We're Not at Home?

Sometimes, children don't disobey at convenient times or in convenient places. In a culture that cannot distinguish between biblical discipline and child abuse, it is unwise to spank children in public. If possible, you should seek a private place to undertake biblical discipline.

When your children are very small, you may choose to overlook things that you would not overlook at home. On balance, this is not a great problem, since most of your training time is spent at home.

Some parents say: "If I do not discipline when we are out of the house, my children will know they can get away with bad behavior when we are not at home." If they are that clever they will remember when you get home. As children near school-age, they can remember events long enough to make correcting them at a later time possible.

It is important to keep the discipline of your children a private matter. If you are in another home, you can ask for a place where you can speak to your child in private.

Being with others when your children are misbehaving is very uncomfortable. You may feel under great social pressure to be successful. You may fear that your relatives expect perfection. You want to be a testimony to them. You want them to see that biblical methods are bearing fruit. The temptation is strong to solve problems through some compromise to avoid embarrassment. But, you may never use your children to promote your convictions. The purpose of discipline is not evangelism. The purpose of discipline is to shepherd your children. Using them to showcase your beliefs abuses their dignity and threatens the integrity of your relationship with them.

When you feel pressure from observers, abandon the scene. Go to a private place where you can respond to your child's needs without the pressure of public observation.

What If I Know My Child Is Lying to Me?

When you feel your child is lying, a good first course is to secure an honest response through discussion. If that fails (and it often will), you need to move to general discussion of the importance of integrity. Remind your child that God requires integrity; that all things are laid bare before him, and that we will all finally give account in his court. Discuss the benefits of integrity in your relationship. Help your child see how he benefits from integrity.

Sometimes, none of this will work. The child remains implacable. What do you do? Do you call him a liar? Never! If you tell your children that you don't believe them, you will dishearten them. If they become persuaded that you will never believe them, there is no reason to talk or for future relationship. Refusing to call your children liars and prizing your relationship with them encourages integrity. I have been amazed at the degree of self-disclosure and even self-incrimination my children have exhibited as a result of this.

If your child will not come clean about what he has done, then he will get away with it this time. That is sad, but your losses and his losses are less if you walk away than if you call him a liar. If what he has done reflects deceit, you will have other opportunities to address it. It is much better to fail this time and preserve relationship than to damage your relationship and fail to address the deceit as well.

What If I'm Not Sure What Happened?

If you are not sure and your child won't tell you, then there is nothing to do. There will be other times when you will be sure of what happened. At those times you can deal with your child's needs. If you are not sure of what happened, how can you secure an acknowledgment from your child (step 3 in the spanking procedure)? How do I know what the issue of the heart is if the situation is ambiguous? Your credibility increases if you will not discipline when things are unclear.

What If Nothing Works?

There are two ways to look at this problem. First, you need to assess whether there are some holes or inconsistencies in what you are doing. Secondly, you need to be prepared to be obedient to God whether or not it seems to bear fruit immediately. It is my experience that most claims that biblical childrearing doesn't work can be understood in one of two ways. Either there is a failure to be consistent in discipline and nuture, or there is some basic lack of integrity in the parent's relationship with God, his child, or both.

What If It Is Too Late?

Perhaps you are feeling, "I'm learning all these things, but my children are no longer five years old or younger." There is no doubt that it is easier to do the job of parenting right than to correct problems. God is powerful, however, and we are never in a situation in which there is no obedient response. I have seen families recover lost ground through patient, honest obedience to God's Word.

This is what you must do:

1. Sit down with your children and explain your new insights. Tell them what you believe you have done wrong in raising them. (Focus on your deficiencies, not theirs.) Help them see how they would have been helped if you had taught them to submit to authority when they were younger.

2. Seek their forgiveness for your failures as a parent.

3. Give your children clear, biblical instruction about the importance of being a person under authority. Help them understand that God has established a chain of command in his world. Show them how living under God's authority is a great blessing. Understanding one's place is like knowing what steps are appropriate in a square dance. The dance is the most enjoyable for all if each dancer knows his place. Always begin any changes you make in your family life with instruction.

4. Give them specific direction about what changes you think are needed in their behavior, attitudes, and so forth. Discuss these things. Help them see how being more submissive to authority will help things to go well with them.

5. Determine how you will respond to disobedience in the future. Be sure that they understand and are comfortable with how you will respond.

6. No new approaches can be successfully undertaken for the sole purpose of changing your children. They will respond to your attempts to be consistently biblical in all of life. They will resist anything that looks to them like manipulation.

7. Whatever you do will require patience. It is hard for a family to change its direction. What is ahead of you is a matter of spiritual struggle against the forces of evil. There is more to it than applying some principles. Pray; seek God's help. Wait on God. Study the Scriptures with your children. Try to take them along with you on your spiritual pilgrimage. Share with them what you're learning and why changes in your family life are important.

Your focus must be on what it means for you to honor God in your family life, not how to get your kids in line. Getting your kids in line is a by-product of honoring God.

Sue and Neal came to Christ when their daughters were five and nine. Their lives had been filled with chaos—living in the world without standards or truth. Sue spent most of her lucid hours on a psychiatrist's couch. Neal worked too many hours, taking frequent comfort in alcohol and drugs. Their daughters grew up without direction—living in a world without walls or any fixed points of reference.

Sue and Neal came to Christ in a large evangelical church where there was no clear biblical teaching about children. They began reading books written by Christian men who accepted many psychological ideas that are not Scriptural. While they wanted to help their girls, things only got worse.

In God's providence, they began to learn some of the principles in this book. They were taught about the heart as the source of behavior and about shaping influences. They started shepherding their girls. They confessed their failure to raise the girls properly. They talked about what God's standards were. They agreed on ways in which their correction and discipline should take new focus. They prayed with their girls. They started having family worship that was oriented toward knowing God, not just reading the Bible together. They showed the love of Christ in their family life.

By God's grace, in the several years that have transpired, their daughters have changed. The girls have begun to understand life in terms of knowing God. They have grown in love for their parents. They have been rescued! It has not been an easy road for Neal and Sue. It is far easier to put in the foundation before you build the house. But, thank God, we are never painted into a corner from which there is no path of obedience.

———— *Application Questions for Chapter 15* ————

1. What Scriptural principles should guide the "when" of using the rod of correction?

2. What elements should be present in the "how" of using the rod of correction?

3. What problem within your children requires the use of the rod of correction?

4. Which of the "most frequently asked questions" were yours?

5. How can the rod provide valuable opportunities to help your children see their need of Christ's work?

6. What would you say to someone who said that spanking is an outmoded concept that robs children of their dignity?

7. Which is easier for you, spanking or talking? How can you avoid imbalance in this matter?

16

Childhood:
Training Objectives

THE DAY ARRIVED for our first child to go to school. We were confident of his success. We had been working on obedience for several years. He had learned to obey us without challenge, without excuse, without delay.

We did all the preparation rituals. We went shopping for all the usual school supplies. We bought a lunch pail and a thermos. We located a book bag his size and furnished it with pencils, erasers, paper, and crayons. We got some sturdy school clothes. We were sure we had prepared him in every way.

We found, to our chagrin, that our preparation was inadequate. We did okay with the shopping trip; it was our training that was inadequate. We had taught our son to obey us. The problem was we weren't there to give direction. There were many situations—on the school bus, during free play time, and in the lunchroom—when he needed guidance. We began to realize that we had to have different training objectives for this new period of his life.

Childhood

I am using the word childhood to refer to the middle period of a child's life. Chronologically, it is ages five to twelve. It is the el-

161

ementary school years. It is the period of time we usually think of when we think about "childhood." It is the time between starting school and puberty.

New challenges confront the parent. The child is developing a growing independence of choice and personality. The child is spending more time away from the direction and oversight of the parents. He is confronted with experiences that parents cannot witness or adjudicate.

Our children are developing a growing independence from us. They think their own thoughts. They have their own ideas about what is fun, what is challenging, and what is worthwhile. Their abilities are defining their interests that express their developing individuality.

One day, when my boys, then ages six and eleven, decided to make a coaster to ride down the hill beside our home, they went to the shed, cut the boards, and assembled their little cart—all without help from me! I was filled with a strange mix of emotions. I was proud of them for being able to do it. Yet, somehow, I was saddened that they could do it without me. I felt strangely displaced.

One Big Issue

Assume that you have taught your child the lesson of stage one. He has come to see himself as a creature made by God, for God. He has come to understand what it means to be under authority. He has learned to obey, without challenge, without excuse, without delay. But your child is now confronted with situations that cannot be reduced to issues of obedience. How do you build on the foundation of submission to parental authority?

Character Development

The big issue during these middle years is *character*. Your child's character must be developed in several areas. You want your child to learn dependability, honesty, kindness, consideration, helpfulness, diligence, loyalty, humility, self-control, moral purity, and a host of other character qualities.

You can't be with him all the time. He must know what to do in situations that you cannot anticipate. He needs biblical wisdom. His conscience must develop as the reasoning factor of the soul so that he will know what he ought to do even when you are not there.

The Change in Focus from Stage One

In stage one the focus was obedience. You were concerned with rooting out the native rebellion of your child's heart. You were concerned that he confront the natural tendency to resist authority. Thus, you addressed defiance and called your child to submission to the authority of God.

Requiring obedience is good preparation, but it does not deal with the issue you must address at this point. The discipline process addresses defiant behavior. What you must address at this point is behavior that is wrong, but not defiant.

Selfishness, for example, is not defiant, but it is wrong. Your child has not left the circle of blessing, but, within the circle, he has shown a crass self-centeredness that is wicked and ugly. Another example would be ridicule. The child can ridicule his brother without necessarily becoming either disobedient or disrespectful to you. The goal is to help him see the ugliness of such behavior.

I recall coming home one day to see my children sprawled on the floor playing a game while my wife ran about trying to do 1,000 simple tasks the children could have done. They were doing something worthwhile. They were not engaged in rebellious behavior. They had not disobeyed their mother, yet I was unhappy with the selfish lack of concern for Mom's busyness. I wanted to see the character qualities of thankfulness for Mother's work and willingness to offer to share the work load with her. If you never address character, you will never get beyond bare obedience.

A Common Sidetrack

I have seen some parents try to solve this problem by making more rules. It is a poor solution. Soon, family life becomes encumbered with more rules than children or parents can remember, let alone follow.

I knew a family that had rules about how long you could use the bathroom in the morning. There were rules about every detail of getting ready for school—right down to the number of strokes of the hairbrush! This may cause you to smile or maybe gasp, but it was an honest attempt to govern family life without addressing character issues. You see, in this family there were four girls and one bathroom. It seemed more manageable to generate rules than to address character issues of self-love, indifference to the needs of others, and so forth.

The problem with this approach, of course, is that it is impossible to make rules comprehensive enough to anticipate every need for direction. In addition, the adult mind is not clever enough to make rules that the child's mind cannot circumvent. More rules won't work!

Imagine that you are riding along in your car. You son has a roll of Lifesavers which he is devouring without offering to share with his brother or sister. He is not being disobedient; he is not exhibiting disrespectful behavior toward you. How can you address him?

Addressing the child's character places the emphasis on issues of the heart. It enables you to get underneath behavior and address the thoughts, motives, and purposes of the heart. For example, "Please share your Lifesavers with your sister" is an issue of obedience. Even a selfish person is capable of isolated instances of sharing. The character issue runs much deeper. God calls for more than isolated instances of sharing. God requires an attitude of heart that gives freely with no thought of return. Addressing character issues gets below the surface to shepherding your children's hearts.

The Problem of Phariseeism
The alternative to addressing character issues in your children is to structure things around rules. You then produce children who learn to keep the rules. They become smug and self-righteous. They

become modern Pharisees whose cup is washed and clean on the outside, but is filthy on the inside.

George, a second-grader in the local Christian school, was an example of this phariseeism. His parents had taught him to obey. In class, he kept the rules. He did his work. He would never speak out or get out of his seat without permission. He was well behaved. The outside of the cup was clean. Inside, George harbored many wicked attitudes. He obviously thought of himself as better than all the kids who needed periodic correction. He was intolerant of being sinned against. He extended forgiveness in a condescending manner. He had no sense of his own sinfulness or need of Christ. He was blind to his selfish and proud attitudes. He was unable to see that even his good behavior required repentance, because it was not a reflection of loving God and others; it reflected pride and self-righteousness.

George's parents were lovely people who loved their son. They had trained him carefully. But, they had dealt with external issues of behavior without addressing the issues of the heart. George saw sin as external things, like not obeying the teacher. He did not see his self-absorbed lack of concern for anyone but himself as sin.

In this middle period of childrearing, we must address the issue of character.

Three-Pronged Tool of Diagnosis

The next chapter explores the "how-to's" of addressing the heart and the conscience. Before we examine the process of addressing the character, we will look at a tool of analysis or diagnosis.

You need some way to look at your children and understand their needs. You need some comprehensive way to organize the things that make up their personalities. You need a grid on which to chart strengths and weaknesses, so that you can zero in on their real needs.

This tool is both simple enough to be useful and comprehensive enough to be helpful. Every six months or so, make this sort of analysis and diagnosis of the needs of your children.

The Child in a Relationship to God

The first prong of analysis is your child in relationship to God. The question is not the personal evangelism question—does he have a relationship with God? The question is what you discern the nature of that relationship to be.

Is your child living in a conscious need for God, and what is the content of his relationship with God? Is he concerned to know and love God? Is God a source of strength, comfort and help? Does he make choices that reflect knowing God? Is he moved by God's ways and truth? Is he alive to spiritual realities? Is there any evidence that he is carrying on an independent (from you as a parent) relationship with God?

Are there false gods before which your child bows? What are the things without which he cannot be happy? What things other than God seem to motivate him? How does he finish the sentence: "What I really want, long for, desire, and esteem is . . ."?

Does he ever talk about God? How does he talk about God? How does he think about God? Is his God small or grand? Does he think of God as a friend, a judge, a helper, or a taskmaster? Is he living out of the fullness of seeing himself in Christ or is he trying to worship and serve himself?

These are not questions about your child's understanding of biblical truth. They are questions about his understanding of the nature of God's grace and salvation through faith in Christ. To shepherd his heart, to lead him to God, you must have some perception of where he is spiritually.

The Child in Relationship to Himself

How does your child think about himself? How well does he understand himself? How aware is he of his strengths and weaknesses? Does he understand his personality? Is he self-conscious about the propensities of his personality?

My friend's daughter, Jennifer, is a person with a tender heart toward the needs of others. Because of this, she can often tell what others are feeling. This is an excellent ability. It makes her sensitive to the feelings of others. There is a downside to this ability. It is easy for such people to allow others to manipulate them. It is easy for her not to tell others how she feels or what she thinks. She is sometimes tempted to let someone else win at a game so that they will not be disappointed.

She must understand these things about herself. If she is to discern these qualities of her personality, my friend must first understand them so that he can help her. Most of us learn these things eventually, but it is often after we are adults. Sadly, some adults never understand the personality issues that drive their responses.

We are complex combinations of strengths and weaknesses. There are things that we can do with ease. There are other things that are painful and arduous. Understanding these things can enable us to shore up our weaknesses and develop our strengths. Your children need to accept and appreciate themselves as unique combinations of strengths and weaknesses—as persons who are exactly what God wanted them to be. Help them to embrace themselves as good enough to do all God has called them to do and has called them to be. In a word, you want them to be content with themselves.

Figure 9 Three Perspectives on Your Child

There is another aspect of your child's knowledge of himself. What attitudes toward himself does he evidence? Is he shy or confident? Is he arrogant or diffident? Is he chained by fears? Is he able to extend himself to others? Does he have a false dependence on others? Does he feel better than others or does he feel inadequate around others?

Harold, a first-grader in my acquaintance, is a relationship junkie. Everything he does is vested with relationship implications. When he sits in the reading circle he is interacting more with those around him than with the reading material. Lining up for recess is a process of jockeying for the recognition of someone. Seatwork time is made meaningful by racing with someone to see who finishes first. (It doesn't even matter whether they know he is racing.) His thoughts about relationships with girls are sexually loaded and laden with baggage a 7-year-old should never carry.

A skillful teacher is helping Harold's parents to understand their son. He is helping them see that Harold is crippled by needing relationships in an idolatrous manner. Harold must understand that only God can slake the thirst of his soul for relationship. Scores of children exhibit clear, lifelong patterns of need that are never understood by them or their parents. They grow up to be enslaved to needs that were evident in seed form in childhood years.

Self-possessed qualities are still another aspect of the child's relationship with himself. Is he able to stick to a task without external props? Is he able to work independently? Is he dependent on the approbation of others, or is he more self-possessed?

You need to understand your child's development in these areas so you can shepherd him. You need to ask the proper questions, to draw out his ideas about himself so that you can point him to Christ in ways that address the thirst of his soul.

The Child in Relationship to Others

What are your child's relationships? How does he interact with others? What sorts of relationships does he have? What does he bring out in others? Are his relationships even or is he always in control or being controlled? Does he fawn for the attention of others?

Is he pleasant with other children his age? How does he deal with disappointment in people? How does he respond to being sinned against? What are areas of relational strength? What are the weaknesses?

In the Christian school, Genny was the take-charge type. She was a born CEO. She told the girls whether their clothes were right. She informed everyone what they should wear to school the next day. If she planned to have braids, the other girls should have braids too. When it was time for recess, she chose the game. Then she chose the teams!

Her teacher understood the issues. She could have told Genny not to be so bossy. But she knew that while Genny might try to obey, eventually the bossiness would resurface. So she chose to help Genny in a better way. She worked with Genny's parents to understand Genny's overbearing manner. Together, they helped Genny to see herself, to see what she was doing to others, to see how she was trying to control people, to see that she was getting comfort for her heart from controlling others. Genny learned how to pray and ask God for help when she was tempted to control others. She was rescued from a life of finding comfort and meaning in controlling others.

Periodic Review

My friend is a manager of a retail business. He understands that his success is not based on what he has to sell, but the skills of his sales people. He, therefore, makes training videos and tries to help his employees to grow. I asked him one day how often each employee in his organization gets a performance review. He said they are reviewed each quarter. I asked him how often he and his wife did a review of his children. He blushed. They never had. I believe his confession is common.

Once or twice a year, you and your spouse should sit down and take stock of your children. Put this simple chart (Figure 9) at the head of the page. Under each category list all your concerns. List also the things you are pleased with. Develop some strategy for dealing with the areas of concern. If you do this, you will prepare yourselves with many fruitful areas to help your children.

In the next chapter, we will look at specific procedures for addressing character development during this exciting middle period of childhood.

——— *Application Questions for Chapter 16* ———

1. How many questions can you generate under each of the headings in our three-pronged diagnostic tool?

2. How often do you sit down and analyze your children in terms of these three issues?

3. How would you articulate the difference between the goals of stage one and the goals of stage two?

4. What are the specific character objectives that you have been pursuing in your school-age children?

5. Have you ever felt, "If I had been there I could have controlled my child, but I wasn't there?"

6. Have you ever kept your child away from an activity because you were afraid he would not be able to handle himself acceptably? What can you do to equip him to function well independent of your presence?

Chapter

17

CHILDHOOD: TRAINING PROCEDURES

*I*T IS A SOUND every parent has heard. Children screaming at one another. The scene, too, is familiar. Two children. One toy.

Every parent has a way of dealing with it. Most ask who had the toy first, reducing it to an issue of justice. Some will holler for the children to "share" or "be nice." Some parents get out the timer. "Okay, you get it for ten minutes and then your brother gets it for ten minutes."

Some disregard the screaming, persuaded that children will fight less if their fights are ignored. Still others console themselves with the timeworn idea that all brothers and sisters fight, therefore it is something they will outgrow.

Most parents walk away from scenes like this convinced that there must be a better way. They wonder if there is some satisfying way to deal with these disputes—some way that addresses the real needs of their children.

What is the better way? You can't simply appeal to the physical—"Do you want a spanking?" You can't simply appeal to the emotions—"I don't like you when you . . . " or "You hurt my feelings when you. . . ." You cannot simply address their love of things—"Do you want me to take your toys away from you?" None of these approaches produce lasting fruit because they do not address the heart biblically. They do address the heart, but these approaches are designed to use the idols of your child's heart as a motivation for acceptable behavior.

Whatever motivates behavior trains the heart. If you motivate with shame you teach your children to respond to shame. If you motivate with emotional appeals you train them to respond to emotional appeal. If you motivate with promises of material things you train them to respond to material incentives. Many of us as adults can see character weaknesses in ourselves that are tied to the motivations offered to us as children.

Addressing the Heart

The temptation is to focus on behavior. Behavior is visible (or perhaps audible). It seems more readily accessible.

Recall with me the principle we saw in the first chapter, *The Heart Directs Behavior*. Behavior is a manifestation of what is going on inside. What a person says or does mirrors the heart. "For out of the overflow of his heart his mouth speaks" (Luke 6:45).

Principles of communication discussed in chapters 8–10 come to life here. Behavior has a "when," a "what," and a "why." The "when" describes the circumstances in which the behavior occurred. The "what" describes the things that were said or done. The "why" describes the internal heart issues that pushed or pulled the specific behavior. You must explore with your children not just the "when" or the "what" of their behavior, but the "why." You must help them to look at the "what" of their behavior from the "why" perspective. Your task is to help them understand the "overflow of the heart" aspect of their behavior.

Carrie was grumbling and complaining one afternoon. It was hard to discern the cause of the problem. Her parents' temptation was simply to address the behavior—"Stop complaining!" or "I don't want to hear another word of complaint from you!" They might have turned to the tried-and-true practice of silencing their child by shaming her—"You should be ashamed of yourself for complaining when you have so many blessings."

Instead, they began to get under the behavior and peel back the layers of excuses and reasons for feeling grumpy. Eventually, they got to the "overflow of the heart" issue. Carrie was mad because things weren't going her way. Inside, she wanted to play God. She wanted to call the shots. She wanted her will to be done on earth as God's will is done in heaven. She had decided how things should go and they weren't going that way. The "overflow of the heart" issue here was being dissatisfied with the job God was doing governing the world. She was not self-conscious of all this, but these were the root issues.

Unless you take behavior apart in this way, you end up always addressing the externals. You will be like the man who tries to solve the problem of weeds in his lawn by mowing the grass. The weeds always grow back.

Appealing to the Conscience

Your children need heart change. Change in the heart begins with conviction of sin. Conviction of sin comes through the conscience. Your children need to be convicted that they have defected from God and are covenant-breakers. They must come to the conviction that the inner man, who relates to God, is an idolater—guilty before God. To help them, you must appeal to the conscience.

As mentioned in chapter 12, we have a pattern for appeal to the conscience, in the ministry of Jesus. He consistently dealt with the conscience, forcing men to judge themselves and their motives. Dealing with character issues requires learning how to appeal to the conscience. If you wish to deal with character and not just with behavior, you must deal with the child in a deep way that enables him to see the implications of his behavior and to indict himself.

In Luke 10, a lawyer (an expert in the Hebrew Scriptures) came to Christ and tested him by asking, "Teacher—What must I do to inherit eternal life?" Jesus asked him how he understood the Law, and he responded with the two great commandments: Love God and your neighbor. Jesus told him he had answered correctly and charged him to obey God's commands. The lawyer then sought to justify himself by asking, "And who is my neighbor?" Christ's challenge was to help this man realize that at any point he was aware of a need, he had an obligation to meet that need. If he failed to, he had broken the Law. Jesus taught this through the story of the Good Samaritan. The story disarmed the man and enabled him to understand how he'd failed. Jesus appealed to his conscience at the end of the story by asking who was a neighbor to the unfortunate traveler. The lawyer moved from asking who his neighbor was to properly assessing who had been a neighbor.

Christ's response to Peter in Matthew 18 provides another illustration of Christ's use of appealing to the conscience. Peter asked for the outer limits of forgiveness. "Lord, how many times shall I forgive my brother when he sins against me?" (Matthew 18:21). Jesus could have said simply, "Peter, if you can ask that question, you don't begin to understand anything about forgiveness." Instead, Jesus told a story that powerfully demonstrated the implication of being one who is forgiven.

In Luke 7, a woman who had lived a sinful life anointed Jesus and wiped his feet with her tears. Simon, a Pharisee, judged Jesus for his lack of discernment. Simon was revolted by the sinful woman. Jesus, knowing Simon's thoughts, told him a story that appealed to his conscience. In the story, there were two men and one money lender. One had a great debt, the other a small debt. Both were forgiven. "Which of them will love him more?" Jesus inquired.

Simon replied, "I suppose the one who had the bigger debt canceled."

"You have judged correctly," Jesus said.

Jesus used the story to indict Simon for his self-righteous thoughts. The appeal was to Simon's conscience. Simon judged himself with his own words. The point of Jesus' story was that this woman loved him more than self-righteous Simon.

You must apply the same methodology to your children's needs. You must get to the root issues by dealing with the conscience. Romans 2:14–15 indicates that the conscience is your ally in teaching your children to understand their sin. The conscience within man is always either excusing or accusing. If you make your appeal there, you avoid making correction a contest between you and your child. Your child's controversy is always with God.

Dealing with children in this way avoids giving them a keepable standard so that they feel smug and righteous. They are faced with God's ways and how much they need the radical, renovating work of Christ.

When your child has come (by the work of the Holy Spirit and the exercise of the means God has ordained for nurturing children) to see his sinfulness, you must point him to Jesus Christ, the only Savior of humankind.

Strive to help your child, who is a selfish sinner, see his need of Christ's grace and mercy in the cross. Dealing with the child's clamor to have the toy first (especially if we have been willing to make "Who had it first?" the issue) without addressing the selfish heart from which it flows, will never lead him to the cross.

Dealing with the real issues of the heart opens the way continually to the cross where forgiveness is found for twisted, warped, and sinful boys and girls. Truly Christian responses cannot be produced legalistically because they deal with attitudes, not just with the external behavior.

Developing Character

It is important to address the heart and appeal to the conscience because of the concern with character development during these middle years of the child's life. Character could be defined as *living consistently with who God is and who I am.*

Training Character

Let's take a character quality like dependability. How does training in dependability fit this definition

WHO GOD IS	WHO I AM
He made me. He placed me here at this time. He is ultimate. I must stand before him one day. I must give account before Him. He has promised to draw near to those who are humble and contrite in heart. He will help me to know His strength and aid. I can know Him and the ability to obey Him. He has promised blessing to those who are dependable.	I am a creature. I have been made by God, for God. He has placed me here at this time and given me these opportunities. I must bring honor to Him. I am made to bring Him glory. As I draw near to Him and seek His face He will enable me to obey Him. I can come to know His help and strength. God promises to give grace to all who call upon Him.

The background material in the two columns above forms the basis for your communication with your child as you help him to learn to be dependable. You want to hold out who God is as a basis for making choices about what he should do and be. His calling as a creature is to be dependable. God does not simply lay it out as a rule to follow, but has sent his Son to change people from the inside out so that they can be what he has called them to be. God will fight alongside of and in behalf of his child. Offer your exhortations and encouragements in a way that is consistent with your child's nature and God's.

You cannot, with integrity, tell your child that if he tries hard enough, if he is good enough, if he really wants it, he can be what God has called him to be. He can't. It is not native to him apart from God's grace and enablement. Nor can you make the more common mistake. You cannot try to build good qualities of character within him without reference to God. Many people conclude that if their child is not a believer, they cannot urge him to his duty in light of who God is.

If you don't call him to be what God has called him to be, you end up giving him a standard of performance that is within the realm of his native abilities apart from grace. It is a standard that does not require knowing and trusting God. In other words, you either call your children to be what they cannot be apart from grace, or you reduce the standard, giving them one they can keep. If you do that, you reduce their need for God accordingly.

You must be willing to hold your child accountable to do those tasks that have been given him to do. Teaching dependability is a process, not an event. It comes through days of patient and consistent rehearsing of the things outlined above. There may be times when this instructional process is underscored with a spanking. But you must commit yourself to patient instruction.

I mentioned earlier that one of my sons went through a period of raising pigs. The hydrant where he secured his water during the winter was a couple hundred feet from the building that housed his pigs. Pigs require a great deal of water. The water had to be carried because a hose would freeze. Carrying this water was a major task each day. It required an hour of carrying for an 11-year-old boy. He would sometimes stumble and spill much of his load. We encouraged him that this job was within his capacity, that it was his duty to take proper care of his animals, and that God could help him to do this job even though it was arduous.

In the years since, I have had two conversations about this period of my son's life. One was with a neighbor who would watch him struggling with his load and wanted to help him. This man thought at the time that I had burdened my son too much. The other conversation was with my son, who has repeatedly said that those days were valuable days for him. They were like David's boyhood days of difficulty with the bear and lion. They had prepared him to do battle with Goliath in the power of the Lord.

David, while only a boy (see 1 Samuel 17:33), said, "The LORD who delivered me from the paw of the lion and the paw of the bear will deliver me from the hand of this Philistine" (1 Samuel 17:37). Why is it that we can see that David learned to trust God in the thick of things as a boy with the lion and the bear, and yet we think that our children cannot learn these lessons of faith as well? What is worse, we set a life before our children that doesn't even require faith. We give a keepable standard that casts them on their own resources and native abilities and endowments—turning them away from Christ and his cross to themselves and their own resources.

Let's think through another character quality. All Christian parents are concerned with moral purity. Remember, character is living consistently with who God is and who I am.

WHO GOD IS

God made me. He owns me. He has created the boundaries for relationships. He has promised great blessing and protection for those who honor Him in their relationships, and has warned of slavery and ruin, which comes upon all those who fail to honor His desires. The relationship that I enjoy for life is to be a picture of His relationship with the church. God gives what He commands. Therefore, He can be known in a way that gives self control.

WHO I AM

I am a creature. I am made by and for a God who is all-wise. I have needs that can only be fulfilled in the context ordained by God. I am called to a lifestyle of fidelity. I am responsible before God for the quality of the relationships that I have. As I honor God, I find completeness in Him and then completeness in the person God has for me. If I dishonor Him or allow myself what He has forbidden, then I suffer irreparable loss of dignity, shame, and degradation.

I am persuaded that we can raise children to be morally pure even in a culture that has exploited sex in every possible manner.

Reading the Proverbs daily provides a very natural setting for discussing moral purity. In Proverbs 5, there is an extended discussion of moral impurity and its fruit, as well as the benefits and sexual delights of purity. The passage warns freely about the danger of becoming ensnared and bound by the cords of sin. The frequent reading of the Proverbs provides scores of opportunities for thinking about the dangers of sexual sin and the joys of sexual freedom within marriage.

Proverbs 7 describes the adulterous woman. It depicts seduction and its results. These passages provide a context for frank discussion of sexuality. They are replete with warning, discernment, and direction.

I have seen children who have understood these issues grow into teens who are circumspect and careful. They are persuaded that God has given the joys of sexuality as well as the context in which it is experienced.

It is important that you let your children in on the fact that there is a sexual dimension to Mom and Dad's relationship. Some Christians have the mistaken idea that their children should never see Mom and Dad in any intimate embrace. The result is that the fraudulent affairs on TV and in the lives of wicked people are the only expressions of sexuality that they ever see. I am not talking about inviting children into the bedroom, but about the importance of them knowing that there is a sexual dimension to Mom and Dad's relationship.

In addition to this instructional role, you must be prepared to address distorted concepts of sexuality that you see expressed in the lives of your children. For example, many little girls learn to walk and sit in ways that are coy and suggestive. Somehow, adults think that being a miniature seductress is cute and they affirm such behavior. Rather, this is a golden opportunity to teach a little girl how and why to handle herself modestly.

The times when young children engage in sexually flirtatious activity are marvelous opportunities to help them form these biblical concepts of sexuality. These are times to talk about what wonderful things are in store for God's people, who can enjoy a life of fullness and joy sexually. It is also a great time to talk about the horrible damage that can be brought on the person who opens himself to sexual experience outside the context that God has ordained.

As children begin to embrace these truths, they develop internal controls against sexual sin. They recognize that sexual exploitation is not the real thing, but a counterfeit of God given sexual enjoyment.

While we have only analyzed two areas of character development, the approaches we have demonstrated would fit any area of character growth.

Interpreting Behavior in Character Terms

We have a couple of problems in thinking clearly about character. One is a failure to see the issues mentioned above. This failure results in not even striving for long-term character development goals. The other pitfall is an inability to work from behavior to the appropriate character issues. This results in seeing only isolated bits of behavior. The result, again, is failure to address long-term character goals.

Parents tend to see their children's behavior in very naive terms. We see the fight over a toy as simply a fight over a toy, when actually it is a failure to prefer others. It is selfishness. It is saying to others, "I don't care about what your wishes are; I want to have what I want." It is a determination to live in the world in a way that exploits every opportunity to serve oneself.

I am not suggesting that this analysis be delivered to your children in the form of a diatribe, but it must be your insight as you seek to shepherd them and help them to see themselves and their needs.

Do you tend to see your children's greedy "I wants" as the idolatry of possessions? Or do you think that it is simply natural—something that will be outgrown? If so, you will fail to help your children grapple with spiritual reality. You will never confront the sinful tendency to find meaning and significance in things. Life does not consist in the abundance of possessions.

Suzie was having a birthday. Anticipating all the money she would get from aunts and uncles, she had begun to plan what she would buy. She was already becoming happy in anticipation of her new things. She was planning whom she would show her new things to and imagining what they would say.

Suzie's parents were concerned that she learn to be thankful for God's bounty. Wisely and gently, they began to address these things. They started by talking about how much she would enjoy the new things she anticipated. Then they began to recall with her how each new thing brings a temporary joy. Suzie could remember times when she had gotten new things that seemed to bring such joy. Together, they observed that while we can be thankful for new things, they quickly lose their luster. They made a list of all the things that Suzie had once been happy to have. Soon, they had such a long list that it was a natural time to stop and pray, giving thanks to God for all he had given. They gently shepherded her heart away from pride in possessions to a more biblical and realistic view of God's blessings.

A Long-Term Vision

You must be a person of long-term vision. You must see your children's need for shepherding, not simply in terms of the here and now, but in terms of long-range vision.

Perhaps the behavior is something common like being a cross person early in the morning. You must think about that cranky, cross behavior not just as an isolated event one given morning, but in terms of life-long impact. When I talk in this way to people, I often hear something like this: "Well, I've never been a morning person either." Perhaps that is true. But the question is this: Has that habit of personality been a blessing or a curse to you?

Being concerned with character will move you from dealing with your school-age children like they are toddlers. I hear people responding to school-age children as if they were 3-year-old kids. They bark commands. Their children are hearing the same old orders but not growing in discernment and understanding. They are not being equipped for the next stage of development—the teenage years.

———— *Application Questions for Chapter 17* ————

1. Can you think of situations in which there is a significant character issue at stake in your child's development, but you are not sure what to do with it?

    Make a project of these situations. Seek to determine what the long-term issues are and how to address them in terms of the issues discussed in this chapter.

2. Can you identify situations in which you have been tempted to give your child a keepable standard because it made things easier?

3. Have you been willing to accept behavior that you required even though you knew the child was not behaving from the heart?

4. How would you articulate the difference between the "when," the "what," and the "why" of behavior?

5. Which is the most significant?

6. Can you give an example of appealing to the conscience?

7. If you were to name five character-training objectives for your son or daughter, what would they be?

Chapter

18

TEENAGERS: TRAINING OBJECTIVES

ELLO, DAD?"
I recognized the voice on the other end of the line, of course. It was my son, who had stopped by my study earlier to borrow the car to go to the mall.

"Hi, what's up?" I queried, trying to sound casual and confident to him.

"I locked the keys in the car," was his nervous reply.

"That's okay. I have another key in my wallet. I'll come over—" Here, I was interrupted.

"Dad, uh, uh, before I locked the keys in the car, I had an accident. Uh, just a little one . . . not too bad . . . I don't think it was my fault . . . Oh, Dad, I'm all right."

One thing you learn about teen drivers is that accidents are always "just little ones" and they are never at fault!

Many folks live in fear of the days when their children will be teens. It's not just the accidents—we've all learned by now that cars are dispensable. Parents live in fear of having teenagers because

183

they fear the alienation which these years seem to bring. They fear having the kind of relationships that they have witnessed between parents and children. We have all heard the little proverb, "Little kids, little problems; big kids, big problems."

Signs of the Times

The benchmarks for this period of life are the onset of puberty and the time when the child leaves home to establish a home of his own.

The teen years are years of monumental insecurity. The youth is neither a child nor an adult. He is unsure about how to act. If he acts like a child, he is chided to "act his age." If he acts like an adult, he is told not to get "too big for his britches." Sometimes, the whole world seems exciting and attractive—he loves being a teen. At other times, it seems frightening, demanding and foreboding—he wishes he never had to face it.

One of our children loved being 17. For him, 17 was the perfect age. You weren't a new driver anymore (you had a few accidents under your belt), but you weren't a legal adult either. Our daughter, facing college and all the decisions that seemed so serious, would hug Mom and Dad and say she never wanted to leave home. She wanted to remain a girl—old enough to do things, young enough to enjoy the shelter and protection of home.

Teens feel vulnerable about everything. They worry about their appearance. Do they have the right clothes? Are they wearing them right? What will their friends think about this shirt, dress, or new haircut? What if they get to wherever they are going and everyone is dressed differently?

They feel anxiety about their understanding of life. Will they know the right thing to do or say in the restaurant? They worry about whether their fund of knowledge is big enough to see them through the situations that they long to experience.

They are unstable in the world of ideas. We have made our dinner table a place for discussing politics, current events, and popular ideas in current discourse. No one has the teenager's capacity to argue on all sides of an idea in a single conversation. Why is this? For the first time he is trying to formulate his independent identity in the world of thought. He knows enough to engage in the conversation, but his ideas are not fully cooked.

Teens feel insecure about their bodies and their appearance. Teenagers spend fully half of their lives in front of a mirror. They worry about whether they are developing on schedule.

Teenagers experience apprehension about their personality. They wonder whether they are serious enough, funny enough, creative enough, carefree enough. One of our children was very straightforward about these fears. He would announce at the breakfast table that he had decided to change his personality. Sometimes he changed personalities more often than he changed his shirts. He didn't know yet that personality is resilient; what he was really reflecting was uncertainty about who he was.

While this is a period of instability, anxiety, and vulnerability, it is also paradoxically a period when children are seeking to establish an independent persona. The teen wants to be his own person. While his need for direction has never been greater, he will resist overt attempts to corral him.

Rebellion

The teenage years are often years of rebellion. Some of the rebellion is simply a misguided attempt to establish individuality. But often, teenage rebellion has deeper roots. In some kids, it is an expression of rebellion that has been latent all along.

Parents sometimes fail to see this. I have spoken with scores of parents who attributed rebellion to the fact the family had moved, or their kids took up with new friends, or they started listening to certain forms of music. While we would readily acknowledge that a family move can be traumatic and that friends can have a negative influence and that some music expresses rebellion, the problem runs deeper than that.

I recall watching a father correct his fourth-grade son. The son was reproved (in front of others) and forced to obey his father. While he obeyed, the grimace on his face disclosed his anger and deep hostility toward his dad. What kept him from open rebellion at that time? Simply this: He was too young and still too intimidated by his dad to dare express the anger he felt. It showed only in his scowl.

Years later, this lad rebelled. He did take up with evil companions. He did listen to antisocial music. But the seeds of rebellion were not sown by rebellious friends. His defiant ideas did not begin with the antisocial lyrics of a pop tune. The rebellion of his heart was an expression of the many times he suffered the indignities of public reproof.

I am always amazed at how quickly defiant teens find each other. The rebellious teen who is new to a school will find the fellow rebels before the first recess. Why is this? A teen falls in with rebellious company because he is a rebel. He does not become a rebel because of the company he keeps.

I am persuaded that rebellious kids may embolden each other, but rarely does a teen who in his heart is willing to submit become rebellious by virtue of the influence of another.

While a child is young, he may feel rebellious at times. He may express defiance on occasion. As long as he is very young and totally dependent upon Mom and Dad, he cannot openly rebel. He still needs Mom and Dad. They still have too much power. However, once he can imagine living on his own without his parents, he begins to give expression to his rebellion. Parents often seem to be taken by surprise, when actually the rebellion has been dormant for years.

Three Foundations for Life

What are parenting goals in this period of life? What can you hope to accomplish? What foundation blocks can you lay that are more solid than your personal ideas? What goals are simple enough to remember, yet comprehensive enough to provide broadly applicable direction?

Proverbs 1:7–19 furnishes you with such direction. There are three foundations of life in this passage: The fear of the Lord (verse 7), adherence to parental instruction (verses 8–9), and disassociation from the wicked (verses 10–19).

My assumption at this point is that parenting has been undertaken according to the model this book sets out. During this period, you desire to see the daily instruction throughout your child's life brought together and internalized by him.

The Fear of the Lord

The first foundation of life is walking in the fear of the Lord. Proverbs 1:7 reads, "The fear of the LORD is the beginning of knowledge, but fools despise wisdom and discipline." Your teen-age child is on the threshold of life independent from you. He is already making choices that have major impact on his life. He is making values decisions each day.

Recall Figure 3. That chart reflected the individual's Godward orientation. It is a split chart because everybody has a Godward orientation. Everyone worships either God or idols. Everyone lives in some sort of fear either of God or idols.

Your teenager must be motivated by a sense of awe and reverence for God. You want the choices he makes to reflect a growing comprehension of what it means to be a God worshiper. Since the question is not *if*, but *what* your child will worship, you must freely confront him with the irrationality of worshiping any lesser god.

Living in fear of God means living in the realization of accountability to him. It is living in light of the fact that he is God and we are creatures. He sees all; everything is open before him. Living in godly fear means living in full light of God as a holy God who calls his people to holiness.

Make it a point to read through the major and minor prophets with your children during their teen years. Your children are part of a contemporary evangelical culture that suffers from a low view of God. Reading the prophets confronts you with a holy God who is awesome and prepared to hold his people to account. I have talked to my teens about the need for a bumper sticker to counterbalance the popular "Smile, God Loves You." This one would say "Tremble, God is a Consuming Fire." Sober your children with the realization that a major theme of more than one third of the Bible (the minor and major prophets) is judgment.

Like any area of theological truth, the key to growth is not the cognitive identification of truth. It is understanding the pertinence of that truth in daily life. You and your children must understand the fear of the Lord in a manner that reorganizes your lives.

You must make the fear of God functional in regular living. For example, teenagers struggle with the fear of man. They worry about what their friends will think of them. They make decisions based on fearing the disapprobation of their peers. Peer pressure is simply living in the fear of man rather than in the fear of God.

What you must do is shepherd your teenagers toward living out of the fear of God rather than the fear of man. You must help them see the relevance of knowing the God who is a consuming fire.

You have to talk with them, helping them to see the ways they are experiencing the fear of man. Then, you must help them understand the bondage that is produced by living for the approval of others. Help them see the futility and idolatry of organizing life around the desire to have approbation. Help them see the true freedom found in a holy indifference to the opinion of others.

Often, the most powerful way these things are taught is by sharing one's own experience. My children were all teenagers when I started doctoral studies at Westminster Theological Seminary. I was pastoring a church and attending classes one day a week. My classes were on Thursday. Each Wednesday night, I would burn the midnight oil. One Wednesday night at about 2 A.M., I was scribbling madly on a legal pad. My wife was strapped to the typewriter, making order of my scratchings. Suddenly, I began to reflect on what I was doing. Here I was, depriving us of sleep. My patient wife was working through the night. In the morning, she would be facing a classroom full of youngsters as a school teacher. She would be exhausted. I would be a hazard on the road as I drove to Philadelphia.

I had to ask myself, "Why am I doing this?" Was I persuaded that God wanted me to deny sleep to my wife and myself? Was I convinced that God's truth and righteousness demanded that I work through the night? No! I was not being driven by the fear of God; I was driven by the fear of man. I wanted the professors to regard me as an efficient, capable pastor. I feared their disapproval. I craved their approval. In my pride and my fear of man, I made choices based on being a man-pleaser, not a God-pleaser. I prayed that night. I confessed my sins to my wife and God. I repented of living in the fear of man.

Sharing this experience with my teen-aged children provided many fruitful times of conversation. They could identify with the choices I had been making. They could see where they had done the same things. They could also see how liberating it was to fear God rather than man.

I am appalled at the skepticism people express about helping teenagers see the importance of the fear of God. It is too often assumed that young people cannot be driven by godly motives.

I am not sure what creates greater skepticism. Is it that teens can know the fear of God, or that parents can teach it? I offer this encouragement: If God wants your children to know the fear of God, then surely those people he has charged with their instruction (parents) can teach it.

The teen who understands the fear of God will be delivered from danger. He will possess wisdom. He will grow in the knowledge of God.

Adherence to Parental Instruction

The second foundation of life is adherence to parental instruction. Proverbs 1:8–9 reads, "Listen, my son, to your father's instruction and do not forsake your mother's teaching. They will be a garland to grace your head and a chain to adorn your neck." Proverbs 6 presents an expanded repetition of this call to walk in wisdom.

My son, keep your father's commands
  and do not forsake your mother's teaching.
Bind them upon your heart forever;
  fasten them around your neck.
When you walk, they will guide you;
  when you sleep, they will watch over you;
  when you awake, they will speak to you.
For these commands are a lamp,
  this teaching is a light,
and the corrections of discipline
  are the way to life (Proverbs 6:20-23).

The young person who adheres to the instruction of his parents will be richly blessed.

It is often assumed that teenage children will find their parents irrelevant. Most expect that by the teen years the parent-child relationship is one of convenience and necessity, rather than choice.

Proverbs holds out a vision of children seeing in their parents a source of wisdom and instruction. It asserts that children will be enriched and greatly benefited by adherence to the values and instruction of their parents. Rather than young people casting off, as irrelevant, their parents' outlook, Solomon directs them to embrace it.

Should this surprise you?

Who should be more relevant to your children? You know them. You know the subtle nuances of their personalities. You know their strengths and weaknesses. You know their life experiences. You understand them. You also know God. You have the Word of God. You know the ways of God. You have struggled and battled to live the Christian life. You understand the disciplines and dangers of Christian living. You understand the world in which they live. You understand the pressures they are now facing. You are committed to them and to God. There is no one who loves them more, who is more deeply committed to them, who accepts them unconditionally. There is no one who will be more honest or more tender. To abandon the instruction and teaching of Mother and Father is lunacy.

If you are living in integrity with God and your children, none of the above is overstated. If you are honestly sharing your life experience and how you have come to know God more deeply and find him more and more satisfying, you are showing the viability of Christian faith.

Your relationship with your children must be honest. You must never give advice that suits your convenience or that spares you trouble or embarrassment. You must be parents who have demonstrated that you are not using your children in any way. If those things are in place, your child will not generally want to remove himself from parental instruction.

Our son, who was in college, was thinking about taking a long weekend off to go on a bicycle tour of about 200 miles. He was six hours away. We never "checked up" on him, yet he called for advice. He had done a fine job of weighing the pertinent details necessary to make a sound decision. He called, however, to run the idea by his mom and dad. Why did he do this? Not because we required it. Not because he was insecure with making decisions, but because he was convinced that we are trusted guides. He also knows that we would not make his decision for him. We would simply help him examine all the important data.

Remaining accessible to instruction is only part of adherence to parental instruction. There is also another important constituent. Adherence to parental instruction also requires retaining the structure of truth in which you have been taught. It means learning to live and work within the *framework of truth* in which you have received instruction.

Aaron was a good example of this. His high school English class was doing a values clarification exercise. An ethical dilemma was posed to demonstrate the relativity of values and the brittle nature of the values the students thought were solid. The teacher posed the ethical dilemma and opened the class discussion. After the class had become completely skewed on the horns of the ethical dilemma,

Aaron offered his suggestion. His suggestion resolved the conflict. Guided by parental instruction, he offered a biblical solution that left the teacher speechless. "Aaron, that's an excellent solution," she murmured. "Your solution was better than the ones offered in the book."

Aaron was helped by adherence to parental instruction. Unhampered by the valueless intellectual climate of our era, he was able to demystify the dilemma. A child furnished with biblical instruction has a firm footing in an academic climate where even the teacher is lost in a sea of no principles or absolutes (see Psalm 119:99–100).

Contexts for Parental Instruction

The primary context for parental instruction is set forth in Deuteronomy 6. It is the ordinary context of daily living. Your children see the power of a life of faith as they see you living it. You do not need to be perfect; you simply need to be people of integrity who are living life in the rich, robust truth of the Word of God.

Whether you are watching a video or playing a game, whether you are doing work or fielding an unwanted phone call, whether you are being successful or smarting from failure—in the ordinary context of daily living, you show the power and viability of Christian faith.

Family Worship

Family worship provides a special context for instruction. There is a temptation to have family worship as a duty. I have known men who lived profligate lives who prided themselves on never missing family worship.

Family worship must connect with the world and life as your teenagers experience it. Family worship must address in lively ways the issues your teenagers face.

Donna is a single mother. She has three adolescent children. Her oldest, a daughter, has become interested in boys. More specifically, boys have become interested in her. Donna was concerned about the relationship that was developing between her daughter and her daughter's boyfriend. The relationship didn't seem negative, but she was concerned. She feared that her daughter would not maintain high standards in her relationship with the young man.

Donna knew that the Word of God is accurate in its descriptions of people and their needs. She knew the promises and warnings of Scripture are well-suited to the needs of all people. She knew that the deepest needs, both of her daughter and the young man, could be met in the context of knowing God's ways. She knew that God's truth is self-authenticating and that it would resonate with this young man and her daughter.

Donna got help to prepare a thorough Bible study on relationships. She and her children and the young man studied the Scriptures together. The kids enjoyed it so much that she had trouble preparing herself fast enough to keep ahead of their regular times of study.

The above story is an illustration of family worship that connects. The family worship addressed the interests and needs of the teens. Donna didn't have to chase after them with the Bible. They sought her out. May we always remember that the Word of God is powerful. Faith comes by hearing and hearing by the Word of Christ.

Disassociation from the Wicked

The third foundational issue is found in Proverbs 1:10. "My son, if sinners entice you, do not give in to them." Solomon is calling his son to disassociation with the wicked. God understands the problem of influence. The one who lives in company with wicked people will learn wicked ways.

While what I have written above is true, it fails to catch the genius of this passage. This passage does not simply tell us to disassociate with the wicked. It also tells us why our children are attracted by such alliances. In verses 10–19 of this chapter, there are over 20 collective pronouns. Note these with me:

"Come along with *us* . . . *we* will get all sorts of plunder . . .
throw in your lot with *us* . . . *we* will share a common purse. . . ."

What is the pitch to the young person in Proverbs 1? It is be-
longing. The attraction of giving in to the wicked is comaraderie.
The appeal is to a very human need to share mutuality with others.
Your kids need to belong.

I was a new elder making a pastoral call early one summer
evening. As I sipped tea and chatted with a middle-aged couple,
their daughter descended the stairs. She was dressed in a tawdry
and immodest manner. As she entered the living room, her father
spoke harshly, "Just where do you think you're going, girl?" he
asked in a voice that would curdle milk. "Out," was the mono-
syllabic reply. "You're not going anywhere dressed like that," he
said, adding, "You look like a slut!" The door closed behind her.
She was gone.

I don't have any idea what happened for the rest of the evening. I
am not sure how long I stayed or what we talked about. All I could
think about was the alienation within the family I was visiting.

No wonder the daughter was leaving home as fast as her legs
could carry her. I didn't want to stay there either.

The most powerful way to keep your children from being attracted by the offers of camaraderie from the wicked is to make
home an attractive place to be.

Young people generally do not run from places where they are
loved and know unconditional acceptance. They do not run away
from homes where there are solid relationships. They do not run
from homes in which the family is planning activities and doing
exciting things.

I made reference earlier to a 650-mile bicycling trip that we took
as a family. That trip was a catalyst for family interaction for nearly
two years. We planned together. We made lists of needed equipment.
We bought bikes and assorted camping gear. We pored over maps,
planning our route. We read books on cycle touring to learn from
others. We trained so we would be physically ready. The children

told their friends about our plans. They felt like they belonged to a special family that was doing unusual things. The cycling vacation provided a sense of unified purpose. It provided a sense of belonging during a critical time in the lives of our three children.

The point is this: The call to association with the wicked comes to our kids. We must work to make home an attractive place to be. Home should be the shelter where the teen is understood and loved, where he is encouraged and shown the paths of life.

These three foundations of life must blow through every conversation with your teens: *The fear of the Lord, adherence to parental instruction, and disassociation from the wicked.* When they do, we can expect the favor of the Lord to rest upon our efforts.

——— *Application Questions for Chapter 18* ———

1. What are the negotiable issues that would enable your teen to express his independence from you in constructive ways?

2. Do you discern any rebellion that may be linked to earlier mistakes in your parenting? What can you do to open discussion of those things?

3. Are you comfortable with helping your child see God as awesome and fearful? How can you explore the implications of Hebrews 12:29 which states that ". . . our God is a consuming fire?"

4. What portions of the Word of God can you read with them to underscore this aspect of God's character?

5. What can you do to provide contexts for parental instruction that is timely for your teens?

6. Are you willing to share your personal experience as a venue for helping your kids think about God's ways?

7. What would be some profitable Bible study projects for you and your teens?

8. Are you providing a home in which your teenager feels loved and accepted? Are his friends welcome in your home, whether they are believers or not?

9. What can you do to provide a special sense of belonging for your children?

Chapter

19

TEENAGERS: TRAINING PROCEDURES

I WENT TO A WEEKEND RETREAT on raising teenagers. My children were almost teens, so I hoped to learn how to prepare for what was to come. The man was a good speaker. He was witty. His presentation was lavishly illustrated by numerous anecdotes drawn from his own experience.

But the retreat left me unsettled. All the stories seemed to be about this father's and his son's attempts to outwit each other. Their relationship resembled a friendly version of *MAD Magazine's* *"Spy vs. Spy."*

I remember thinking that if keeping my children in line depended on me outwitting them, I might fail. I am now persuaded that raising teenagers is not a matter of out-maneuvering them. It is much more exciting and satisfying than that.

Internalization of the Gospel

Internalization of the gospel is the process of your children embracing the things of God as their own living faith. Your wish during this period is to see your children develop autonomous identities as persons under God.

It is obvious that internalizing the gospel requires the work of the Holy Spirit in the child. No parent can do that work; nor can you produce it through your labors. You labor, however, in the hope that God honors his covenant and works through means. While you dare not presume upon his sovereign mercy, you may labor with expectation that the gospel is powerful.

Your heart's desire in every phase of childrearing is to see your children internalize the gospel. The desire in all your training, in all your entreaty, in all your correction and discipline, is to see your children come to the place where they have embraced the claims of Christian faith.

The reason for shepherding their hearts—appealing to the conscience, focusing on character issues in correction and discipline, addressing the heart as the spring of life, and refusing to give them a keepable standard that would eliminate their need of Christ—is to see them come to know God. You want them to recognize their need of God, to embrace Christ, and to see their life in light of the Kingdom of God.

Internalization is the fruition of all that we have considered. Recall with me Figure 3 that illustrates Godward orientation. Internalization is your children coming to maturity as persons who know and worship God.

I've often been asked whether I thought my children would be Christians. Parents desperately seek some promise from the Bible that their children will have faith. I don't believe that promise is found in the Word of God.

I have been asked, "Don't you think that if you raise your children the right way, God has promised to save them?" If such a promise existed, it wouldn't comfort me. I haven't raised them well enough.

Looking over their lives, I want to join the ranks of parents who would like to do it over again. I am keenly aware of shortcomings and limitations.

It should be clear by now that I am not talking about "getting them saved" in terms of an evangelistic event. I rather envision leading them along the path of a deepening understanding of and commitment to God. Repentance toward God and faith in the Lord Jesus Christ will be a part of that life of deepening understanding of and commitment to God.

You have reason for hope as parents who desire to see your children have faith. The hope is the power of the gospel. The gospel is suited to the human condition. The gospel is attractive. God has already shown great mercy to your children. He has given them a place of rich privilege. He has placed them in a home where they have heard his truth. They have seen the transforming power of grace in the lives of his people. Your prayer and expectation is that the gospel will overcome their resistance as it has yours.

Most books written about teenagers presume rebellion, or at least the testing of the limits of parental control. My assumption is the opposite. My assumption is that you have carried out your parenting task with integrity and that your children, in the words of Titus 1:9, "are not open to the charge of being wild and disobedient."

If you are disheartened, feeling that your teens are unruly and that you are already in grave trouble in your relationship, I refer you to what was said earlier. Turning to God in repentance with your family, and setting new goals, will, in God's mercy, bring you to a reconciliation. Seek God who can make what is crooked, straight.

I have had the joy of seeing families work through times of great pain and family travail during these teenage years. God has given them grace and integrity to seek him during their long night of suffering and has brought a new day of joy and peace. They can now labor in God's Kingdom in solidarity with their once-rebellious children.

Shepherding the Internalization of the Gospel

Your role during this period is a shepherding role of encouraging the child and seeking to influence him in the process of internalizing the gospel.

You have taught your child about God. You have shown him the character of God. You have proclaimed God's glory. You have held before him the blessings of living under God's protective care. You have spoken of the chief end of man: "Glorifying God and enjoying him forever." You have warned him about the dangers of not loving and trusting God. In the natural credulity of childhood, he has accepted what you have told him.

In his teen years, he is receiving new input. He has a growing realization of his own sin and brokenness. He has accepted the standards he has been taught. Now, in his growing self-awareness, he is confronted with his inability to do what he ought to do. He has not become worse than he has been all his life, he is simply more self-conscious of his weakness and need.

He is also confronted with a growing realization that everybody does not believe as he has been taught. He reads books, hears, and learns things that challenge everything he has been taught to believe.

Your task as a parent is to shepherd and nurture his interaction with the gospel. What will enable you to have access to this teen who is growing into an adult?

Developing a Shepherding Relationship with Teens

I am assuming that you have successfully dealt with the first two stages of your child's development, and that the Holy Spirit has worked through those means, so that your role is not remedial, but directive. You have established your role and right to be involved in your child's life. That is simply an aspect of the agency you exercise as a parent under God. Your son or daughter already recognizes your authority.

If your authority over your teen is not established, you must take the time to seek God and work back through your life with your teen. Confess, rethink, and establish your authority and your son or daughter's responsibility based on God's Word to both of you. There is no shortcut to your right as their shepherd or your teen desiring to be shepherded. The only route to those things is repentance and faith.

Your concern to be a constructive force in your child's life has been established and demonstrated as you have sought to deal with his character in the middle years of childhood. Your shepherding now is simply an extension of those previous roles in your child's life.

Authority Vs. Influence

One of the foundational elements of shepherding is influence. Recall this figure from Chapter 10:

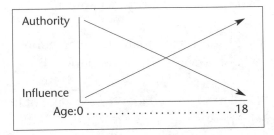

Figure 6 Authority/Influence Continuum

Authority in this chart denotes what may be accomplished with your child because you are stronger, faster, larger, and so forth. Influence represents the willingness of your child to place himself under your authority because he trusts you. Your role as an influence is one of helping him to know his needs and be honest with himself.

For example, your teenage child is impossible to live with. She is always snapping at everyone in her way. If you are trying to wield authority, you may lay down the law. "I don't ever want to hear that again . . . you are grounded for the month . . . you can't talk on the phone . . . I won't have that around my house!"

By contrast, if you are seeking to influence, you will move toward her with the gentle reproofs of life. "I see you are having a problem with being a pleasant person. I love you and I want to help you learn to speak in ways that are constructive."

The one approach increases the sense of alienation and drives the teen toward associations that may be harmful. The other approach moves toward the child in love and gentle rebuke. It embraces and accepts. It urges the child to accept correction as a wise person. It doesn't make the child feel like a fool. Personal indignities must not be the condition upon which we rebuke our children.

As a parent seeking to shepherd, you want to influence your child to respond to things that are reasonable, drawn from insight into human character based on Scripture. You are seeking to influence and provide counsel. You can accomplish nothing of lasting value simply by being an authority. You must seek to counsel and influence.

My 16-year-old son came in late one afternoon. It had been a day off from school because of a heavy snowfall.

Son: "Dad, can I go sledding for a couple of hours with the neighbors?"

Father: "Well, son, you have been gone for several hours and there is a project in your room that you need to complete."

Son: "I thought I would do that later. I can do that in the dark, but I can't sled in the dark."

Father: "I am concerned about something. I see this project in your room as something that you began to do several weeks ago and have not completed. That concerns me, because I think you leave projects incomplete more often that you should. You have a great attitude toward anything your Mother or I ask you to do, but the long-term tasks that require you to pace yourself through them seem to be hard for you to do."

SON: "I'm too busy. By the time I get done with school and wrestling practice, there isn't time to get to it."

FATHER: "Well, I know you are busy, but today is a free day and you didn't get to it. I don't think that is good for you. I would like to see you overcome your aversion to long-term tasks. I'm just concerned about you, son."

SON: "I can accept what you are saying, Dad, but I think I could go sledding and still get that work done."

FATHER: "Okay, son. You know what you need to do."

I noticed a few minutes later that Aaron was still at home. "Aren't you going sledding?" I inquired.

"Yes, but I decided to do this work first."

That's all there was to it. No yelling, no threats, no hurtful talk. Why did he decide to stay? He thought that I had a valid point, so he stayed to follow through on our talk. He was willing to be influenced by me.

I am convinced that there are few times when a parent must demand that teens do or don't do something. In the cases where every day is made up of demanding and requiring, parents have not practiced biblical principles. The son or daughter who is expected to respond to demands and requirements is probably circumventing them and doing what he or she desires anyhow.

Shepherding through Doubt

There will be time of doubt and question in the life of any young person raised in a Christian home. Part of internalization is becoming self-conscious of faith. Every young person goes through some period in which he examines the claims of Christian faith at "arm's length."

Every teen must come to grips with whether he has believed for himself or been swept along by the family. He will have times when he questions the validity of Scripture. He will need to strengthen his grip on the cardinal truths of the faith.

Sometimes, parents are tempted to panic when their children have questions. They respond with things like, "I can't believe you are doubting God," or "You just have to believe it," or "It is best not to question those things."

Encourage your children not to run from their questions. Everyone does not have to have every question, but everyone must find resolution for the questions he has. Christian faith is robust enough to stand close scrutiny.

You will sometimes have to help teens find answers to problems that you have never found difficult. You may need to educate yourself. I have needed to learn some basic physics in order to help my children look at this discipline from a biblical perspective. You may have to help them locate books or other apologetic materials.

You can share your own experience of dealing with questions of faith. You can show them that non-Christian philosophy is devoid of satisfying and unified answers to the major philosophical questions about humankind and the cosmos.

We have also exposed our children to relationships with people who understand the world of ideas through the grid of biblical faith. Developing family relationships with Christian people who have interests in common with our teens is important for our children. Our children have been enriched by relationships with Christian people who are much older than they. These relationships have buttressed our instruction and strengthened our influence.

Above all, don't panic during these times. Walk through them with your kids, entrusting them and your training and their salvation to Almighty God.

Positive Interaction

You must maintain a positive relationship with teens. Your interaction should have the objective of ministry. Be a constructive force in the life of your child. You want to be a source of encouragement and inspiration.

That is not always easy. Teenagers are capable of colossal blunders. There is an enormous gap between the teen's desire to be autonomous and his understanding of life. This is fertile soil for gigantic mistakes. It is easy for a parent to lose his focus.

One summer, our son was using our second car for transportation to his summer job. He came home one afternoon with the rear bumper tied on with a rope. Naturally, I was curious. It seems that as he rounded a bend in the road, a pencil rolled from the dashboard onto the floor of the car. The bumper "fell off" when he reached down to pick up the pencil and hit a guard rail!

We had a "parts car" at this time, so my son said he would fix the car. That night he removed the ruined bumper, but he didn't have time to replace it with the one from the "parts car."

The next day he backed into a mountain during a three-point turn. It probably would not have done much damage if the rear bumper had been on the car. . . .

During times of failure like I have recounted above, your teens need positive interaction. You need to keep your eye on the goals you have for your children. They need Mom and Dad to be constructive and creative. You need to have a proper sense of proportion, remembering that your child is worth much more than a car.

I am not talking about shielding them from responsibility. I am not talking about insulating them from the effects of their errors of judgment. Those are important lessons when handled constructively. What I have in view is parental interaction that is full of hope and courage. This interaction is able to turn a fiasco into an opportunity to learn and go forward.

You cannot afford to berate your teens with destructive speech. The young person who is told he is "worthless, no good, a loser, a slob, or a bum," will probably live up to his parents' expectations.

The Proverbs tell us that pleasant words promote instruction. "The wise in heart are called discerning, and pleasant words promote instruction" (Proverbs 16:21). Pleasant words grease the wheels of instruction. A later verse underscores the same lesson:

"Pleasant words are a honeycomb, sweet to the soul and healing to the bones" (Proverbs 16:24).

It is no wonder so many teens do not receive instruction from their parents. They are suffering under the cruelty of their parents' harsh words. Any instruction is lost to a wounded spirit and deepening alienation.

"A wise man's heart guides his mouth, and his lips promote instruction" (Proverbs 16:23).

In all your interaction, your focus is to see your teenagers find comfort and strength in knowing God.

Teenagers experience frequent failure. As Christian parents, you must become adept at taking your child to the Cross to find forgiveness and power to live. You do your children great disservice if you strip away all the excuses for failure and force them to see their sin as it is, without giving them well-worn paths to the Cross. No wonder Christian teens often have such a poor self-concept! They have been taught to see through all their false mechanisms for dealing with guilt, but have not been taught adequately where to go with it.

Even your times of warning must have a positive thrust. You have a good pattern in the book of Hebrews. In Hebrews 6, after giving very straightforward warning, the writer adds these words: "Even though we speak like this, dear friends, we are confident of better things in your case . . ." (Hebrews 6:19).

Developing an Adult Relationship

A good metaphor for the parent and teenage child relationship is the relationship adults would have with one another. There are several elements to an adult relationship that parallel your relationship with your teen. This does not signal the child's moving out from under parental oversight; rather, it marks the parent's sensitivity to the child's ascent into adulthood.

Think of your relationship to your child in these terms. In your nurturing relationships with adult friends, how would you try to pursue that friendship? What are some of the "dos" and "don'ts" of adult relationship?

Waiting for the Right Time

In regular friendship relationships, you would never jump on your friend the moment you saw him do something you questioned the wisdom of, or thought was wrong. So long as his life was not endangered, you would not pounce on him about everything you saw him do or heard him say. You would bide your time, waiting for the proper moment. Do your teenagers need less consideration?

I have been embarrassed sometimes to be with the parents of teenagers and hear them reprimand their children over every little fault. You have no biblical obligation to censure your children for everything they do that is irritating to you. You must increasingly make room for your teenager's differing style and manner, holding correction for moral and ethical failures.

When you have determined that you must address some issue with your children, you must watch for a good time. If you have an important issue to discuss, it helps to take a walk or jog, or a ride in the car to provide some uninterrupted time for a good conversation.

Develop sensitivity to your children. Sometimes, they are very talkative. At other times, they are less forthcoming. During the times when they are accessible, you must be prepared to engage them. This may be inconvenient for you, but it is crucial to your relationship with them.

Deal with Broad Themes

In adult relationships, you do not nitpick your friends over every little thing that needs attention. Rather, you look for broad themes of response. You try to understand the patterns of response and that's what you talk about.

In the earlier illustration with my son's project, the broad theme was sticking with long-range tasks. The project in his room was illustrative of other things. That is why I mentioned it, and that is why he responded as he did. What I said resonated with him. He made the connections because he saw the pattern in himself when I drew it to his attention. He didn't fight it because he didn't have to deal with my anger or disapproval. It was easy (in comparison to the alternatives) to respond to my direction.

Allowing Room for Disagreement

In adult relationships, it is possible to disagree with each other and remain friends. The same should be true in your relationships with your children. They don't have to agree with you on everything in order to respect you.

Sometimes, parents fail to distinguish between what is Scriptural and what reflects their personal taste. In things such as dress, hairstyle, and so forth, it is possible for honest people to disagree. There are many areas in which you need to draw in the reins and give clear direction to your teens. Don't waste your influence on things that don't matter. That may mean they wear some bizarre costumes from time to time. Don't worry—people will forget and their faltering and experimenting will settle in time. They needn't be carbon copies of you to be godly!

Beyond Internalization

Even the internalization process is not the end. It simply opens the way for the future development of your children. Remember, you want to see them taking their place as autonomous individuals under the Lord. That will involve the following:

1. Developing a Christian mind. Your children need to develop the ability to think Christianly. They need to learn to dissect any area of thought and subject it to biblical critique.

Heather had a research paper to write. Her subject was child abuse. She chose her sources, including some that espoused a Christian perspective. When she had completed the paper, she brought it to us for inspection. We rejoiced to see that her conclusion was a Christian critique of the problem and solutions that reflect that Christian faith is the only source of deep and final healing.

2. Developing friendships with adults. There are two elements of this.

A) Making friends with adults within the church and community.

B) Developing nurturing and constructive friendships and relationships among their peers.

3. Discovering and developing their peculiar ministry niche. This involves understanding how God has equipped them to contribute to his people. It will also entail a deepening sense of mutuality with others and becoming established corporately with the people of God. You cannot make this happen. You can only hope to shepherd the process.

4. Determining a career in which they can fulfill the cultural mandate and God's command that they support themselves and share with others in need. Your role here is to facilitate their understanding of their strengths and weaknesses. Suppress the desire to make them into what you want them to be. Help them make choices that will bring them success in what they want to be.

5. Establishment of their own home and family identity as a member of the society and a part of the church of Christ. You can help them guard the integrity of their new family relationships. Practice godly wisdom in your expectations of them. Let go of that part of your previous relationship. Your relationship must change for them to establish a home and family before God. Remember, the parent-child relationship is temporary. The husband-wife relationship is permanent. "For this reason a man will leave his father and his mother (temporary relationship) and be united to his wife, and they will become one flesh (permanent relationship)" (Genesis 2:24).

6. Development of a mature relationship with parents. This involves a relationship of mutuality and, as God's providence allows, shared ministry.

Entrusting Your Children to God

The parenting task comes to an end. We are no longer the on-site shepherds. That aspect of our relationship is done. This will be true whether they marry or just take their place as an adult in their community. God intends for parenting to be a temporary task.

In the final analysis, you must entrust your children to God. How they turn out will depend on more than what you have done in providing shaping influences. It will depend on the nature of their Godward commitment. Ultimately, you leave them to God, knowing that you can entrust your children to the God who has dealt so graciously with you.

Application Questions for Chapter 19

1. If you find your relationship strained, what can you do to promote understanding and healing? Are there things that you must repent of and seek forgiveness for?

2. Are you using gentle reproofs and pleasant speech to influence your teens with insights drawn from the Scripture?

3. Have you learned to shepherd your teenager through periods of doubt and confusion about faith? Are you willing to help them explore their questions and confusion?

4. What are good times for you to address things with your teenager? When do you find openness and receptivity to interaction?

5. Are you consciously raising your children to leave? Does your vision for shepherding blend into a relationship of mutuality with adult children?

Scripture Index

211

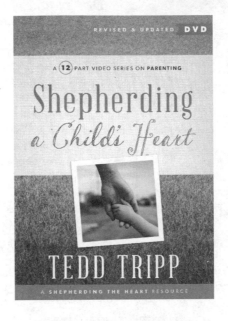

"Don't Make Me Count to Three!"

A MOM'S LOOK AT HEART-ORIENTED DISCIPLINE

"Don't Make Me Count to Three!"

GINGER PLOWMAN

Through personal experience and the practical application of Scripture, Ginger encourages and equips moms to reach past outward behavior and dive deeply into issues of the heart.

Her candid approach will help moms move beyond the frustration of not knowing how to handle issues of disobedience and into a more confident, well-balanced approach to raising their children.

Available at Amazon or Shepherd Press

Now Available
Six Week Study Guide

Wise Words for Moms
iPhone, iPad App

Take *Wise Words for Moms* with you everywhere!

My child is complaining…or fearful…or selfish. How do I help him?
Wise Words for Moms lists heart-searching questions to ask your child, then directs you to Scripture with God's encouragements for change.

Features:
• Link to ESV or *YouVersion* Bible
• Note-jotting capability
• Add Scripture passages you find

Available at Apple App Store

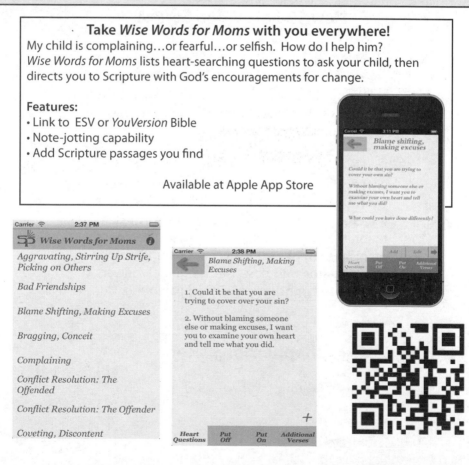

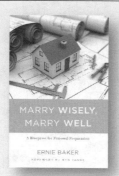
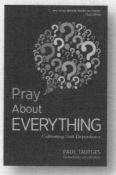